T3-BOE-529

BRESCIA COLLEGE LIBRARY

3 6277 00005869 5

Student Loans in Canada

Past, Present, and Future

Ross Finnie
and
Saul Schwartz

with comments by
Bruce Chapman, Paul Davenport,
and Harry Hassanwalia

BRESCIA COLLEGE
LIBRARY
65832

Observation 42

C.D. Howe Institute

C.D. Howe Institute publications are available from:
Renouf Publishing Company Limited, 5369 Canotek Road, Unit 1,
Ottawa, Ontario K1J 9J3; tel.: 613-745-2665; fax: 613-745-7660

and from Renouf's stores at:
71½ Sparks Street, Ottawa; phone (613) 238-8985
12 Adelaide Street West, Toronto; phone (416) 363-3171

For trade book orders, please contact:
McGraw-Hill Ryerson Limited, 300 Water Street,
Whitby, Ontario L1N 9B6; phone (416) 430-5050

Institute publications are also available in microform from:
Micromedia Limited, 20 Victoria Street,
Toronto, Ontario M5C 2N8

This book is printed on recycled, acid-free paper.

Canadian Cataloguing in Publication Data

Finnie, Ross
    Student loans in Canada : past, present, and future

(Observation, ISSN 0826-9947 ; 42)
Includes bibliographical references.
ISBN 0-88806-402-0

1. Student loan funds – Canada. I. Schwartz, Saul,
1951– . II. C.D. Howe Institute. III. Series:
Observation (C.D. Howe Institute). English ; 42.

LB2340.4.C2F56 1996   378.3′62′0971   C96-932233-X

© C.D. Howe Institute, Toronto.
Quotation with appropriate credit is permissible.
Cover design by Leroux Design Inc.
Printed in Canada by Printcrafters Inc.,
Winnipeg, Manitoba, December 1996.

Contents

Student Loans in Canada:
   Past, Present, and Future,
   by *Ross Finnie* and *Saul Schwartz*

Figures

Tables

Foreword

Canadians know from their own family experiences that the more educated their children become, the more likely it is that they will find good employment. Therefore, the ability of students to pay tuition for postsecondary education is an issue that should pre-occupy us all. As universities scramble to cope with government cutbacks, there is increasing pressure on students to pay a greater share of their education. At the same time, the old ways of providing assistance to students seem to be seriously flawed.

In this comprehensive analysis, Ross Finnie and Saul Schwartz take a detailed look at the workings and experience of the Canada Student Loans Program, the primary federal program for delivering financial assistance to postsecondary students; the increasing financial pressure on students; and the portion of their education costs that students actually pay and how that has been changing. Finally, the authors explore a new, and perhaps a better, way of getting financial help to students: the concept of income contingent repayment student loan systems. Within the larger picture of the quality of postsecondary education, its cost and its effectiveness, financial assistance for postsecondary students is an important element that we must get right.

Rounding out the volume are comments on the main study by Bruce Chapman, Paul Davenport, and Harry Hassanwalia.

The volume was copy edited by Lenore d'Anjou and Barry A. Norris, and prepared for publication by Wendy Longsworth. The analysis and opinions presented in the study are the responsibility of the authors, and do not necessarily reflect the views of the members or Board of Directors of the C.D. Howe Institute.

Thomas E. Kierans
President and
Chief Executive Officer

Acknowledgments

The research reported herein was funded in part by Human Resources Development Canada, Applied Research Branch, Human Capital and Education Studies Division. Professor Finnie also gratefully acknowledges the Social Sciences and Humanities Research Council of Canada for a Strategic Themes Research Grant for this and related work on the school-to-work transition.

We appreciate helpful comments received from John Richards. Staff at Human Resources Development Canada (Monty Woodyard, Gerry Godsoe, and Jean Wright) also provided many useful suggestions. We also thank C.D. Howe Institute staff (Barry Norris, Wendy Longsworth, and Susan Knapp) and copy editor Lee d'Anjou for editorial and production assistance of a high standard. Top-quality research assistance was provided by Gaétan Garneau.

Ross Finnie and
Saul Schwartz

Student Loans in Canada:
Past, Present, and Future

Ross Finnie
and
Saul Schwartz

Chapter 1

Introduction

Just when the opportunities for finding a good job and embarking on an interesting and rewarding career seem to depend more than ever on having an advanced level of education, the Canadian postsecondary education system is in a state of fiscal crisis, largely because of deep and continuing cuts in government transfers. These dynamics, relatively recent as they are, have already led to troubling questions about what universities and colleges should do, for whom they should do it, and the means by which their missions should be financed. Of the many issues relating to these questions of purpose and means, this book focuses primarily on student borrowing through the Canada Student Loans Program (CSLP).

The student loans system is a timely subject for at least two reasons. First, for the past 15 years, governments have been shifting some of the costs of postsecondary education over to students by increasing tuition fees, and this trend continues in the wake of new federal and provincial cutbacks. In Ontario, for example, university fees rose by 20 percent between the 1995/96 and 1996/97 academic years. This mounting financial pressure on students makes it appropriate to evaluate the financial aid system in terms of its ability to deliver assistance to those in need in the most efficient manner possible and to consider any need for reform.

Second, the CSLP, the primary federal program for delivering financial assistance to postsecondary students, has recently undergone several major changes. In the following pages, we both describe this "New CSLP" (our term) and explain the basic structure of the "Old CSLP" (again, our term) as it existed before the 1994 reforms, providing an empirical record of borrowing and repayment patterns under that system. We also make some proposals for further reform. The work should, therefore, be of interest to many people concerned with student loans and related public policy: students, teachers, university administrators, policymakers at both the provincial and federal levels, and individuals interested in the future of postsecondary education in Canada.

Financial Pressure on Students

As noted, much of the current interest in the student loan system unquestionably stems from the recent increases in tuition fees and the resulting financial pressure on students. It is thus useful to provide some documentation of these trends and to place them in historical perspective. To this end, Figure 1 shows the ratio of tuition fees to instructional costs from the early 1970s into the 1990s, while Figure 2 shows the trends in tuition levels alone over the same time period.

For the next 15 or so years, tuition rates grew more slowly than government transfers, and the ratio of tuition to instructional costs fell to a low of about 18 percent in 1980. During the next decade, however, tuition rates began to rise faster than government transfers, increasing the students' share. And with the accelerated tuition increases and government cutbacks of the 1990s, the ratio has climbed rapidly. Thus, recent sharp movements have left the ratio of tuition fees to total instructional costs at approximately the levels that prevailed in the early 1960s.[1]

The pattern for tuition levels themselves is roughly similar. Adjusted for inflation, tuition generally declined through the 1970s,

---

1 This ratio is meant to measure how much of the costs of postsecondary education are paid for by tuition fees. The issue is quite complex, both conceptually and in terms of measurement problems (what exactly are "instructional" costs and how are they to be measured?). But in the absence of better indicators, the tuition-to-costs ratio is a useful indicator of the broad trends in which we are interested. Another measure is the ratio of tuition fees to operating revenues. Stager (1989, 31) estimates that tuition fees made up about 30 percent of university operating revenues in the early 1960s.

Figure 1: *Ratio of University Tuition Fees to Instructional Expenditures, academic years 1972/73 to 1993/94*

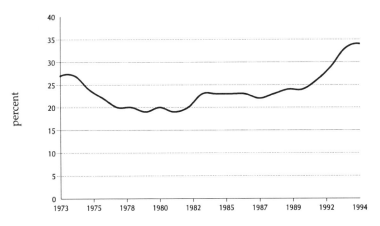

Source: Canadian Association of University Business Officers, *Financial Statistics of Universities and Colleges* (Ottawa: Statistics Canada for the Canadian Association of University Business Officers), various years.

trended upward very gently during the 1980s, and have risen sharply in the 1990s. Currently scheduled increases — including hikes of 20 percent in Ontario and 35 percent in Alberta — will generally return the levels to those of the early 1960s. These recent tuition increases, together with massive cutbacks in provincial student grant programs, have, not surprisingly, led to commensurate surges in student borrowing (see Appendix A).

Thus, although what tuition levels *should* be is an open question — one we address briefly in Appendix B — rates are now higher than at any time since the early 1960s (and still climbing), represent a higher proportion of instructional costs than at any time in the last three decades, and have left students under greater financial pressure than at any time in the recent past. Hence, an evaluation of the student aid system appears appropriate regardless of other policy issues concerning postsecondary education that may be raised in the years to come.

Figure 2:   *Tuition Fees, academic years 1971/72 to 1993/94*

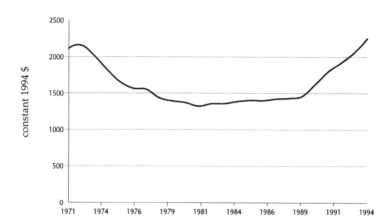

Source: Association of Universities and Colleges of Canada, using data from Statistics Canada.

The Old CSLP

Since its inception in 1964, the CSLP has been an integral part of the college and university experience for many Canadian students. By fiscal year 1994/95,[2] 2.4 million of them had borrowed a total of $10.6 billion (Canada 1996a, 2-71). Having thus enhanced the educational opportunities of generations of Canadians, the CSLP takes an important place in the list of institutions that help define Canada, contributing to the nation's human resource base as well as helping to bring postsecondary education within reach of all those with the will and ability to attend.

By the late 1980s and early 1990s, however, this venerable institution had become increasingly subject to criticisms: that some students were receiving too little aid while others received too much; that default rates were too high, leading to excessive costs to the federal government; and that repayment terms were too inflexible, causing undue hardship for students.

---

2 Unless otherwise specified, the noncalendar years mentioned here that refer to CSLP reports are the program's fiscal years. Those that refer to its rules are academic years.

Our description of the Old CSLP sets the stage for presenting, in Chapter 3, the results of an empirical investigation of borrowing and repayment patterns. Using the National Graduates Surveys (NGS), we analyzed the experience of three cohorts of postsecondary graduates — those who graduated in 1982, 1986, and 1990. In particular, we looked at the probability of graduating with a student loan, the total amount borrowed, the burden of student debt (as measured by debt-to-earnings ratios), repayment rates as of two years after graduation, and reported repayment problems. Most of the results relate to level of education, gender, major field of study, and cohort, but we also examined how borrowing and repayment patterns vary with province, socioeconomic background (as proxied by parental education), and selected aspects of the educational experience. This analysis thus provides a solid empirical basis for the other sections of the study.

The New CSLP

Then, in Chapter 4, we summarize the significant changes the CSLP has undergone in the past few years.

First, borrowing limits have been raised substantially in the first real increase since 1984. Second, need-assessment procedures have been significantly revised and, for the first time, will operate almost uniformly across all provinces except Ontario. Third, the interest-relief program has been extended to borrowers who have low incomes. Finally and most important, the government is no longer guaranteeing new student loans. Through an agreement reached after lengthy negotiations, financial institutions are accepting responsibility for collection of the loans and for the risk of default, in return for a government payment of 5 percent of the value of loans going into repayment. Provincial authorities will continue to determine who gets a loan of how much, but they will use the standardized eligibility criteria.

We organize our discussion of these changes around the criticisms of the Old CSLP.

ICR Loan Programs

Finally, in Chapter 5, we discuss the concept of income contingent repayment (ICR) student loan systems, an idea that has taken on new life as criticisms of the existing loan system have mounted. ICR comes in many forms, but its defining characteristic is that the rate of repayment depends on earnings in the postschooling years. Advocates suggest that ICR can provide a more equitable, more flexible, and more efficient system of delivering student financial aid.

Many supporters of higher tuition fees couple their proposals with parallel calls for the adoption of an ICR loan system, the two having a certain logical connection and policy synergy (because flexible repayment rates may reduce the burden of a given amount of borrowing, thereby softening the impact of the expected tuition increases). ICR and tuition increases have thus become linked in the current policy debate. We consider ICR and tuition increases as two quite separate issues, however; one can have ICR without tuition increases, and one can have (as, indeed, Canadians have had) tuition increases without ICR.

Conclusion

In the concluding chapter of the book, we offer a summary assessment of the New CSLP and a series of policy suggestions that are intended to guide further reform in the years to come. We find the potential of the New CSLP extremely interesting. It is, for example, almost certain to reduce the number and cost of loan defaults simply by shifting the incentives for collection over to the financial institutions that hold the loans. Similarly, the flexible repayment terms that make ICR so attractive to many may evolve naturally as banks and students negotiate mutually acceptable repayment schedules.

Chapter 2

The CSLP through the Early 1990s

Since its inception in 1964, the Canada Student Loans Program (CSLP) has been the principal vehicle for delivering federal financial assistance to postsecondary students in Canada.[1] In its old form, the program's principal function was to guarantee loans made by private financial institutions (mostly banks) to postsecondary students who qualified for assistance according to their assessed need. In addition, the program paid the interest on loans while the student was in school and, until recently, for six months following graduation. Finally, the CSLP was responsible for making payments to provinces and territories that had opted out of the federal program, for providing administrative funds to those that participated, and for coordinating and developing federal policies and program in the field of student assistance.

The Operation of the Old CSLP

Until its recent reform, the CSLP had been operating with little change for many years. Even the limits on loans had barely changed since 1983.

---

1 Through the first years of the 1990s, the provinces received substantial federal assistance as part of Established Programs Financing (EPF) transfers, some of which were directed to postsecondary *institutions*. In contrast, the CSLP was — and is — a means of providing federal aid to *individuals*.

Assessment Procedures

Although the CSLP is a federal program, eligibility for loans was —
and still is — based on need assessments carried out by provincial
authorities. These procedures have begun with the calculation of
direct educational costs (such as books and tuition) plus allowances
for living costs and related expenses. Costs are then compared with
the estimates of the student's resources — savings from a summer
job, contributions on the part of the student's parents, scholarships
and bursaries, and other resources to which the student has access.

Within each province, the need-assessment formulas have been
based primarily on standard estimates of costs and resources, not on
actual amounts. Using standardized estimates simplifies application
procedures and treats students in similar situations in like manner:
two individuals with comparable family incomes and comparable
education costs are eligible, in principle, to borrow comparable amounts.

In operation, however, the use of standardized assessment
procedures inevitably results in similar treatment for students in
quite different circumstances. For example, two students whose
parents have similar incomes may be eligible for a loan of the same
amount even though one of them receives more financial assistance
from his or her parents than the other. The two students have
significant differences in *actual* need, but *assessed* need — and loan
eligibility — is the same in the two cases. Nevertheless, attempting
to assess students' true needs on a case-by-case basis — delving into
the individual's and the family's personal finances and spending
habits — would probably be prohibitively expensive and unaccept-
ably invasive.

Until very recently, the provinces had significantly different
need-assessment procedures and their own methods of combining
CSLP loans and provincial assistance. For example, in some provinces, the federal loans were offered first, with remaining needs
addressed by provincial grants. An important exception was Ontario, where provincial grants were offered first, followed by CSLP
loans made available for those with greater need. Thus, students
with the same assessed need but from different provinces could

receive different combinations of federal and provincial funds, as well as different proportions of grants and loans (see Appendix A).

The provinces have also determined which institutions were eligible for student loans. Virtually all colleges and universities have been certified, but there has been considerable variation in the treatment of vocational institutes, especially those in the private sector.

Borrowing Limits

The Old (and the New) CSLP set loan limits, expressed in terms of the maximum amount that a student could borrow for each week of school. The limit was $50 per week in the early 1980s, rose to $100 per week in 1983, and $105 in 1984, and then remained frozen until the CSLP reforms of 1994 (which raised it to the current $165 per week). For a typical 34-week school year, the maximum amount that could be borrowed in 1989/90 thus was $3,570. This limit was not intended to ensure that students' assessed need — let alone their actual need — was met.

Repayment and Default

Under the Old CSLP, a student was to have agreed with a bank on a repayment schedule and an interest rate and begun loan repayments within six months of leaving school. CSLP loans had a maximum fixed payment period of ten years,[2] regardless of the actual size of the loan or the former student's financial situation. Interest rates varied from year to year. Hence, monthly payments varied greatly from one situation to another.

The interest rate the student paid was based on a set of calculations made each August. The "student rate" for all loans consolidated over the following 12 months was fixed at the return on five- to

---

2 Actually, given the six month interest-free grace period, the amortization period was nine and a half years.

ten-year government bonds over the previous six months plus one percentage point for administrative costs.[3]

These preferential interest rates constituted another important form of subsidy, beyond that embodied in the federal loan guarantee and the government's payment of interest while the student was in school. Individuals with the limited earnings records and the lack of collateral that characterize recent school leavers would normally expect to pay considerably higher interest rates for a personal loan.

To ease repayment burdens, interest rate relief was available for the unemployed with low family income for periods of three months at a time, up to a maximum of 18 months.

If the loan fell into default (generally as a consequence of a series of missed loan payments), the bank claimed from the federal government reimbursement of the principal plus accumulated interest. If the CSLP accepted the claim, it paid the bank, took over responsibility for the loan, and attempted to recover the unpaid balance, usually by employing a private collection agency.[4] Other measures included legal action by the Department of Justice and the withholding of income tax refunds to set against outstanding balances.

Default rates have varied over time and by the characteristics of students but have averaged out to approximately one borrower in five. The fact that a loan was in default does not, of course, mean that it would never be repaid. The collection agencies employed by the CSLP recovered some of the loans, and it carried more on its books for a considerable period of time before declaring them unrecoverable. According to the CSLP, the "loan loss" rate (the proportion of the total amount borrowed that has been declared unrecoverable) has been 7 percent (Canada 1993, table 13).

---

3 The "minister's rate," which the government paid loan holders while the student was in school, was based on a similar formula but used one- to five-year bond yields instead of the longer-term bonds used to calculate the student rate. That latter rate was truly preferential: for example, 9.00 percent in academic year 1994/95, 8.625 percent in 1993/94, 9.5 percent in 1992/93, and 10.6 percent in 1991/92. Interest rates on credit cards are generally in the 15 to 20 percent range.

4 As a result, the largest single contract for collection services in Canada involved the CSLP (conversation with CSLP officials, December 1995).

An Overview of CSLP Finances

In the 1994/95 academic year, the most recent for which figures are available, CSLP loans were negotiated by 317,000 students, almost all of whom (more than 99 percent) were enrolled full time. The total value was $1.2 billion. Average loan values had been gradually rising, and the year's average of $3,337 represented an increase of about 20 percent over the amount negotiated in 1990/91, three years earlier.[5]

The average cumulated CSLP indebtedness of those receiving loans has begun to rise as well. In 1994/95, 43 percent of all borrowers had total borrowing of less than $5,000, 78 percent less than $10,000, and 93 percent less $15,000. In 1990/91, the corresponding percentages were 58, 84, and 95.[6]

Roughly 70 percent of all loans went to students under the age of 25, and 86 percent to students under 30. About 53 percent of the loans were issued to university students, 35 percent to college students, 12 percent to those attending private vocational training schools, and 1 percent to those at other institutions. As for regional variations, the percentage of undergraduate university students taking out CSLP loans varied from a low of 27 percent in Manitoba to a high of 52 percent in Newfoundland. All of these figures were similar to those of preceding years.

In 1994/95, there were approximately 82,000 applications for interest relief for the unemployed, representing about 52,000 individuals (some applied more than once). Of these, about 45,000 individuals received assistance, representing an approval rate of 86 percent and resulting in expenditures of $15 million.

Table 1 sets out the total CSLP expenditures and offsetting revenues for 1994/95.

---

5 The figures in this subsection are taken primarily from the 1996/97 Main Estimates for the Department of Human Resources Development (Canada 1996a, 2-23 and 2-71–2-77). The figures in the first three paragraphs are estimates only.

6 These totals do not, of course, represent *final* debt loads, since many students would take out further loans in subsequent years. The 1990/91 numbers are from Canada (1995, 5–45).

Table 1:   CSLP Revenue and Expenditure, fiscal year 1994/95

	Amount	% of Total
	(current $ millions)	*(%)*
Revenue		
Repayment through collection agents	103.5	86.0
Repayment through income tax withholding	16.9	14.0
Total	*120.4*	*100.0*
Expenses		
Claims paid on defaulted loans	201.7	38.1
Interest subsidies	193.5	36.6
Collection costs on defaulted loans	20.8	3.9
Interest relief	15.1	2.9
Payments to Quebec and Northwest Territories (as nonparticipating jurisdictions)	93.8	17.7
Loans forgiven because of death or disability	4.3	0.8
Total	*529.2*	*100.0*

Source: Canada 1996a, 2-72.

Mounting Criticisms

Despite the success of the CSLP in delivering financial assistance to generations of needy students and thereby enhancing the educational opportunities of millions of Canadians, it has never been without its critics. Their criticisms appeared to gain force and become more focused in the late 1980s and early 1990s, particularly after disapproving comments in the federal auditor-general's 1990 report (Canada 1990)[7] and the release of a consultant's report commissioned by the CSLP itself (Bennecon 1991).[8]

---

7 It criticized the CSLP in no uncertain terms for "a lack of monitoring of activities administered by the provinces, a high number of defaults, a lack of success in recovering loans, and a lack of proper management information" (Canada 1990, 696).

8 Other critical evaluations of the period included a study by the Association of Universities and Colleges of Canada (AUCC 1993); representations by student groups (Duncan 1992; 1993; Students Union of Nova Scotia 1994); and work by academics (Stager 1989; Stager and Derkach 1992; West 1993).

Mounting fiscal pressures also contributed to the pressure for change, as the federal government looked for ways to cut its spending in all areas.

Too Little Borrowing, Too Much Borrowing

One major criticism of the CSLP was that some students seemed unable to borrow enough, while others could borrow too much. On the one hand, the maximum loan limit — frozen at $105 per week of school from 1984 through 1993 — became increasingly inadequate as tuition rose over the same period. Students who had limited access to other financing faced a growing gap between their educational costs and the resources available to them. One presumes that such students were left to make do with less or to abandon their post-secondary schooling.

Simultaneously, there was a perception that certain students who did not really need CSLP financing were able to obtain loans — with the public subsidies contained therein — to replace funding that could and should have come from themselves or their families. Such students, it was said, spent their loan money in ways not intended by the program — on cars, holidays, stereos, and the like. These criticisms naturally pointed to problems with the need-assessment procedures.

Excessive Default Rates

The second major criticism of the CSLP was that default rates seemed excessively high, driving up the costs of the program because of the government's role as guarantor of student loans. There was also a perception that some students were defaulting not so much because of dire financial straits but simply as a convenient means of evading repayment of their loans.

In a 1993 document, the secretary of state reported that about a fifth of all CSLP loans were taken over from the lending institution because of default. Of these, about one-third were eventually collected, another third were deemed potentially collectible, and a final third were likely to be ultimately written off as uncollectible. Thus, as already noted, the loan loss rate was about 7 percent (Canada 1993, table 13). The auditor-general had also judged the costs of collection efforts to be quite high, ranging "from 19 to 28 cents for every dollar recovered" (Canada 1990, 703).

Since the issue of default rates has become central to the debates regarding the CSLP, let us examine the most recent evidence from a somewhat different perspective, basing the discussion on the 1993/94 program year, the most recent for which final figures are available.[9] Restricting the view to student loans that had been issued to those who were no longer in school — and who were thus at risk of being in default — one finds that there was a total of $7.4 billion in lending from the inception of the CSLP through July 1994, compared with approximately $1.6 billion paid out in default claims (principal and interest) up to that date. The gross cost of defaults, therefore, amounted to 21.4 percent of all lending.[10]

Offsetting these claims paid out, however, were collections on defaulted loans, which totaled approximately $0.7 billion (again, including principal and interest), or 41 percent of the value of all claims. Net losses due to default over the period covered therefore amounted to approximately $0.9 billion ($1.6 billion minus $0.7 billion), or 12.6 percent of the value of all loans issued.

These figures are only meant to be illustrative, and are inherently imprecise because of the dynamic nature of the processes being studied. That is, some of the loans that had not yet gone into default would eventually do so, while additional money would be collected on some defaults that were still being pursued. Furthermore, collection costs would have to be figured into any full calculation of the

---

9 The numbers used in this section are drawn from Canada (1995, 5-36–5-46).

10 Since the claim total includes both principal and interest due the initial lender, the figure given does not represent the percentage of actual borrowing that had gone into default. The calculation would require knowing the amount of actual principal that had been defaulted on. Unfortunately, this information is not available, so all we can say is that the figure would be lower than the 21.4 percent cited.

costs to the the government (see below). Nevertheless, the 12.6 percent figure is a useful indicator of the historical magnitude of the net cost of loan defaults to the CSLP as of the mid-1990s.

Approximately 30, 895 claims were paid in 1993/94, with an average value of $5,655 per claim paid, which was 16.9 percent higher than in 1990/91 (the number of individuals making claims remained relatively stable throughout the early 1990s). Of all claims paid, 63.6 percent were for amounts under $5,000, and 85.3 percent were for amounts under $10,000 (again, including principal and interest).

The most recent evidence on defaults under the Old CSLP might therefore be summarized as follows: a fairly large proportion of student loans (about 20 percent) went into default, but a significant proportion of the value of these loans (about 40 percent) was subsequently collected. Thus, the overall loss due to default was perhaps in the range of 10–12 percent of all borrowing.

Individuals may default on their student loans because their earnings are lower than expected, because they did not appreciate the full consequences of their borrowing when it was undertaken, or because they experience some adverse event, such as difficulty in finding a job or unanticipated family responsibilities.[11] Part of the default problem under the Old CSLP, however, seemed to be related to some actual features of the structure of the program. First, defaulting on a student loan could not affect a borrower's credit record since CSLP regulations forbade releasing this information to credit bureaus — thus significantly reducing the consequences of nonpayment.[12]

Second, the relatively small size of student loans and the below-market interest rates they carried diminished banks' incentives for

---

11 The next section offers some evidence on self-reported repayment problems, and we find that the size of the loan and postgraduation earnings patterns do play an explanatory role.

12 The auditor-general noted, "[t]he fact that students do not repay loans has no impact on their credit rating since this information is not released to credit bureaus" and suggested that it was at least partly for this reason that "44 percent of defaulting borrowers have been located but do not co-operate in repaying their loans" (Canada 1990, 701).

pursuing repayment, with this unfavorable calculus clearly exacerbated by the almost automatic reimbursement for loans that went into default. The auditor-general's report was quite damning in this regard: "[O]ur audit found that, in the majority of cases, banks have made little effort to encourage repayment by students" (Canada 1990, 701).

Finally, the repayment terms were quite rigid. Most students faced a standard repayment period and payments set only by the extent of their borrowing. Given the uncertain economic fortunes that often characterize the period after leaving school, it was inevitable that some of those who experienced spells of low earnings or unemployment would be unable to meet their loan payments. Any flexibility that a financial institution might have been inclined to show toward such potential defaulters was discouraged by a CSLP rule that departures from the standard schedule put the bank's loan guarantee at risk. Furthermore, the same factors that reduced the banks' incentives to pursue collection (the relatively small size of the loans, the below-market interest rates, and the guarantees for those that went into default) also reduced their incentives to manage loans on an individual basis with more sensitivity to circumstances.

Discouragement to Borrowing

The same inflexible repayment terms that may have encouraged excessive default may also have discouraged some students from borrowing in the first place. Some individuals who needed to borrow undoubtedly recognized the possibility of encountering an uncertain economic situation immediately after leaving school. The specter of heavy debt burdens and inflexible repayment terms may have caused them to not borrow up to their limit or to delay, discontinue, or simply not undertake postsecondary studies.[13]

---

13 See Duncan (1992; 1993) and the references provided there for discussions of these and related points.

Chapter 3

An Empirical Analysis of Student Borrowing and Repayment

In this chapter, we report the results of our empirical investigation of the borrowing and repayment patterns of graduates of Canadian postsecondary institutions.[1]

The Data and Analysis

Our analysis is based on three waves of the National Graduates Surveys (NGS), representing those who left Canadian colleges and universities in 1982, 1986, and 1990. For each cohort, information was gathered during interviews conducted two and five years after graduation.

The NGS data bases are large (each cohort comprising approximately 16,000 university graduates and 8,000 college graduates) and were designed to represent the underlying population of postsecondary graduates in each of the three years covered.[2] Response rates were about 80 percent for the first interview and 90 percent for the second, which is quite good for a survey of this type.

---

1 This chapter is largely based on Finnie and Garneau (1996a; 1996b) and Finnie and Schwartz (1996), which can be consulted for more detailed discussions of the material presented here.

2 The NGS employed a random sample design stratified by province, level of education, and field of study. The results reported here reflect the corresponding sample weights.

The NGS files include information on graduates' educational experiences, early labor market outcomes, and sociodemographic characteristics. Moreover, the NGS data bases contain several variables related to student borrowing that were constructed from information gathered at the first interview (two years after graduation). These variables include the amount owed at graduation, the amount still owed two years after graduation, self-identified problems with making loan repayments, and the reasons for any such problems.

The ability to match this loan information to individuals' other attributes, the abundant size of the samples, and the cross-cohort nature of the three files available make these NGS data uniquely well suited for the study of student borrowing in Canada. As a result, the work summarized here represents the most detailed analysis of student borrowing and repayment patterns to date.

The Samples and Variables Used

Except in one specific section of the analysis (as noted), we restricted our samples to graduates who did not receive a second degree or study full time subsequent to graduation so that we could focus on those who had finished their studies without mixing in the record of those who continued on. We had two main reasons for defining the samples in this way. First, those who continued their studies after graduation continued to accumulate debt, so that we could not observe final debt levels, the precise times of graduation, or post-graduation earnings. Second, the field of study, which is an important element of the analysis, was not identified for 1982 graduates who obtained another degree.

For largely technical reasons, we also limited the 1982 and 1986 samples to those who had responded to both the two-year and to the five-year postgraduation interviews.[3]

---

3 This limit was necessitated by the fact that the 1986 file used for this analysis included only graduates who responded to both interviews. We dropped one-time interviews from the 1982 sample so that it would have the same structure...

We verified the key loan variables for consistency and dropped or corrected a small number of records.[4] Earnings figures were also checked, and a few problematic observations eliminated.[5] Finally, we omitted from specific calculations observations for which the required information was missing. All dollar amounts for loans and incomes were converted to constant 1990 values.

The outcomes we analyzed included the following:

- whether or not the individual graduated with a loan;
- the size of the loan;
- the debt-to-earnings ratio;
- the proportion of the loan repaid by two years after graduation; and
- reported difficulties with repayment of the loan.

The Framework of Analysis

Our discussion is based on two sets of results. One is a series of cross-tabulations of the overall patterns of borrowing and repay-

---

Note 3 - cont'd.

...as the later file, thus ensuring comparability of the two sets of results. The 1990 graduates had been interviewed only once, so the same selection rules were not possible across all three files. Fortunately, the small attrition from the first interview to the second meant this problem was not great.

4 In one case, for example, total borrowing and the amount owed at graduation were listed as $5,000, but the amount of debt outstanding two years later was given as $40,000; we adjusted the latter figure to $4,000, deciding that that amount was reasonable and that the manner in which the response had been recorded on the questionnaire made such an error quite possible. If we judged an observation to be substantially inconsistent and there was no obvious correction, we dropped it. Smaller inconsistencies were left untouched (to avoid biasing the sample by an excessive trimming of errors in one direction only). About 80 observations for each cohort were checked in this manner. Approximately one-quarter were corrected, one-quarter dropped, and the rest left unchanged.

5 Those with earnings of more than $500,000 as of the first interview were eliminated from the sample if this amount differed dramatically from the earnings level given in the second interview or the previous year's income if that was available. Full-time, full-year workers who reported earnings of less than $5,000 per year were also dropped.

ment, beginning with the patterns for men and women by broad level of education (college, bachelor's, master's, PhD) for all three cohorts. For example, we show the proportion who graduated with a student loan and the average level of borrowing for each gender-education group for each cohort. Next, we break the findings down by field of study. Finally, we report detailed distributions by gender and level of education — for example, the percentage of college, bachelor's, master's, and PhD graduates with loans of less than $1,000, with loans of from $1,000 to $5,000, and so on. The relevant tables and graphic representations of some of the results are included in the text.

In order to provide a more detailed view of the various factors related to borrowing and repayment, we also discuss our findings from a multivariate econometric analysis of the borrowing and repayment patterns of the bachelor's graduates. The regression results allow us, for example, to distinguish among the independent influences of field of study, province, and socioeconomic background. The key regression results are reported in Appendix C.[6]

The Effects of Recent Changes

How does our historical analysis stand up in light of recent changes in tuition and in student aid programs, both federal and provincial? As already noted, tuition fees have risen significantly since 1990. Moreover, borrowing limits under the Canada Student Loans Program (CSLP) have increased substantially, while provincial student aid is now more often granted in the forms of loans rather than grants (see Appendix A). As a result, student borrowing has increased substantially in the past few years relative to that of 1990 graduates, who are the most recent cohort we studied. Thus, the experience of those who have borrowed in this decade cannot be directly observed in our results, and the reader is cautioned against extrapolating too far forward from our findings.

---

6 The full analysis is in Finnie and Schwartz (1996).

Despite that important caveat, the NGS data used here have the virtue of being the most recent available. For anyone who wishes to inspect the empirical record, they are the best to be had. Furthermore, many of the findings here are similar across the three cohorts studied and thus seem to represent stable patterns that are likely to have continued in more recent years. In short, although one would always like to have more recent data, the analysis based on the NGS data used here should remain interesting and relevant.

The Empirical Findings

The NGS data enabled us to provide detailed answers to the following questions:

- What proportion of graduates took out government student loan program (SLP) loans for their postsecondary schooling?[7]
- What amounts did they borrow?
- How did the amounts borrowed compare with earnings levels two years after graduation?
- How much had been repaid within two years of graduation?
- What proportion of graduates had difficulties with the repayment of their loans?
- What were the characteristics and circumstances of those experiencing such problems?
- What differences were there in borrowing and repayment by province, by socioeconomic background (as proxied by parental education), by various aspects of the educational program (co-op, part time, normal length of program), and by marital status? How did these patterns differ by gender?
- What were the trends over time?

---

7 The NGS data do not distinguish between loans from federal and from provincial governments. During the period under consideration, however, CSLP loans were by far the most important (see Appendix A).

The Extent of Borrowing
from Student Loan Programs

The proportion of graduates who finished their studies with a student loan and the average amount those with loans borrowed are shown in Table 2. The patterns are also presented graphically in Figures 3 and 4.

Of the most recent cohort, roughly a quarter to almost a half finished their studies with a student loan outstanding, with the rates varying by degree level. The mean amounts borrowed also varied by that level, with college graduates averaging about $5,500 and university graduates $7,500 to $9,000.

The trends over time are interesting. The incidence of borrowing at the college level rose fairly sharply from 1982 to 1986 and then remained approximately stable; men and women of the classes of 1986 and 1990 all had borrowing rates in the low 40 percent range. The average amounts borrowed followed similar trends across the three cohorts, rising to more than $5,500 by 1990. Among bachelor's graduates, the proportion who had borrowed dropped slightly from 1982 to 1986 and then edged back up in 1990 for both men and women. The mean amounts borrowed rose substantially between 1982 and 1986 (probably because of the increase in loan limits instituted in 1984) and then moved up further in 1990 to more than $8,500.

As for graduate students, those at the master's level also increased their overall borrowing over time, but the composition of those increases differed from that for the college and bachelor's students. The proportion of master's borrowers held roughly steady across the three cohorts, while the mean amounts borrowed rose for both men and women.

For male doctoral graduates, the trends were quite different. The proportion who finished school with loans *dropped* significantly over the three cohorts; for the 1990 cohort, it was 27 percent — the lowest rate for all the education groups analyzed here. Nonetheless, average amounts borrowed *rose* moderately across time (to a mean of $7,570 in 1990).

Table 2: *Incidence of Student Borrowing and Mean Amounts Owed at Graduation, 1982, 1986, and 1990*

	Gender	1982		1986		1990	
		Incidence (%)	Mean ($)[a]	Incidence (%)	Mean ($)[a]	Incidence (%)	Mean ($)[a]
CoLege/CEGEP	Male	34	3,480	41	5,380	42	5,520
	Female	36	3,400	43	5,190	43	5,890
Bachelor's	Male	46	5,410	44	8,240	47	8,660
	Female	41	5,120	39	8,110	44	8,710
Master's	Male	32	5,900	34	7,700	32	8,440
	Female	31	5,830	31	6,890	32	8,640
PhD	Male	42	6,010	30	6,140	27	7,570
	Female	33	7,110	28	5,330	28	8,970

[a] Constant 1990 dollars.

Figure 3: *Incidence of Borrowing at Graduation, 1982, 1986, and 1990*

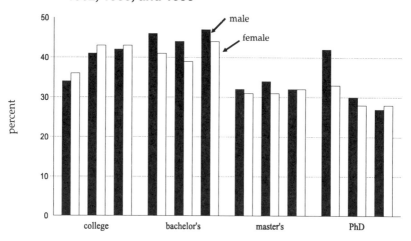

1st bar = 1982 cohort   2nd bar = 1986 cohort   3rd bar = 1990 cohort

Source: Table 2.

There were also reductions in the proportion of women who received PhDs with loans. Although these declines were not as great as men's, women's rates had been lower to begin with, leaving them at a level comparable to men's in 1990. The average amounts borrowed by female PhD graduates first dropped and then increased substantially, so those in the first and third cohorts had mean loans higher than their male peers.

In summary, the overall level of student borrowing for graduates rose at all education levels except the PhD. The detailed pattern of the increases, however, differed from group to group.

Some Preliminary Conclusions. The apparent absence of a gender borrowing gap—men and women borrowed roughly similar amounts — is interesting since men generally earn more than women, even among postsecondary graduates. Because of this gap in earnings, the similar loan levels were bound to translate into greater repayment burdens for women (as measured by debt-to-earnings ratios).

Figure 4:   *Mean Amounts Owed at Graduation,*
1982, 1986, and 1990

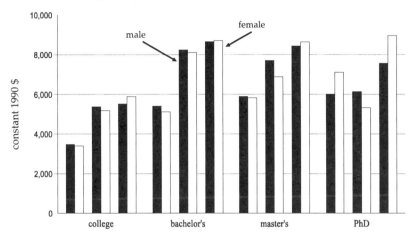

1st bar = 1982 cohort   2nd bar = 1986 cohort   3rd bar = 1990 cohort

Source: Table 2.

Simultaneous changes in the proportion of those borrowing and the mean amount borrowed need to be interpreted carefully. An increase in the number of borrowers in which "new" borrowers took out less (which is quite plausible) would represent an unambiguous rise in borrowing but could result in a *decline* in mean borrowing. In general, both rates and average amounts need to be considered. A useful measure of overall borrowing consists of multiplying the incidence of borrowing by the mean for those who borrow.[8]

To some observers, average borrowing of $5,000 to $9,000 may not seem high. These amounts are, for example, generally less than the price of even the least expensive new car currently on the market

---

8 For the 1990 cohort, this measure of average borrowing across *all* graduates, including nonborrowers, yields: college, $2,320 for women and $2,530 for men; bachelor's, $4,070 for men and $3,830 for women; master's, $2,700 for men and $2,770 for women; and PhD, $2,040 for men and $2,510 for women. We calculated this measure for the other cohorts (but do not show the results). In almost every case, overall borrowing rose monotonically from 1982 to 1986 to 1990, for PhD graduates, however, overall borrowing dipped in 1986 and then rose again in 1990.

and may seem especially reasonable in light of the advantages that typically accrue to postsecondary graduates in terms of their employment and earnings (perhaps now more than ever). Others, however, may find these levels of borrowing worrisome and be particularly concerned with the increases over time. The borrowing levels are, as noted, surely higher among more recent graduates than those covered by our data. Moreover, the numbers describe *average* borrowing; as we show later, there have already been real problems for the small group of graduates who had run up substantial levels of debt but ended up with significantly lower than average earnings or were unemployed.

A Deeper Look. Readers can begin to investigate the patterns of borrowing more deeply by looking at the patterns by major field of study for the three cohorts of bachelor's graduates, shown in Table 3.[9] In general, borrowing was fairly similar across the different fields of study, with no obvious patterns in the proportions of graduates with loans or the average amounts borrowed. Male graduates in the medical and health group (almost exclusively doctors) are an exception because they are in school for a greater-than-average number of years. (For more on the patterns by field, see the discussion of the regression results below.)

Table 4 provides a different manner of probing, a look at the distribution of the amount borrowed for the most recent cohort. The spread was quite wide. Sizable numbers of graduates in each gender/ education group had relatively small overall loans of $5,000 or less and the clear majority had less than $10,000, but many individuals borrowed as much as $20,000, and a smattering even more.

These distributions are interesting on a descriptive level and also mean that any analysis of student borrowing based on the "average" student can be very misleading.

---

9 Borrowing by field of study for college, master's, and PhD graduates is reported in Finnie (1994). The results are broadly similar to those found for the bachelor's graduates discussed here.

Table 3: Borrowing by Field, Bachelor's Graduates, 1982, 1986, and 1990

Field of Study	Gender	1982		1986		1990	
		Incidence	Mean	Incidence	Mean	Incidence	Mean
		(%)	($)[a]	(%)	($)[a]	(%)	($)[a]
Education	Male	40	6,380	42	8,240	56	9,500
	Female	49	5,560	41	8,500	47	8,860
Fine arts & humanities	Male	46	4,970	44	9,110	44	8,210
	Female	33	5,050	35	8,130	41	7,360
Commerce, economics, law	Male	42	5,030	37	8,780	44	8,900
	Female	44	4,680	36	7,660	45	9,070
Other social sciences	Male	42	4,400	39	7,770	41	7,430
	Female	31	4,490	38	7,590	36	7,810
Agriculture & biosciences	Male	50	5,090	45	7,880	49	8,920
	Female	46	5,580	57	8,910	50	9,060
Engineering	Male	52	5,150	55	7,170	55	7,830
	Female	39	4,790	51	5,230	55	8,820
Medical & health	Male	75	9,120	66	11,450	58	12,570
	Female	47	5,200	42	8,440	49	10,240
Maths & physical sciences	Male	39	5,050	37	6,640	42	7,910
	Female	37	4,420	37	7,150	42	9,020

[a] Constant 1990 dollars.

Table 4:   Distribution of Amounts Borrowed, 1990 Graduates

	Gender	Less than $1,000	$1,000 to $4,999	$5,000 to $9,999	$10,000 to $14,000	$15,000 to $19,999	$20,000 to $29,999	$30,000 or more
					(percent)			
College/CEGEP	Male	5	43	38	10	2	1	0
	Female	4	38	43	12	3	1	0
Bachelor's	Male	2	29	28	27	10	4	1
	Female	2	24	32	29	9	4	1
Master's	Male	2	27	34	21	10	4	1
	Female	1	25	35	26	9	3	1
PhD	Male	2	39	29	18	7	3	2
	Female	1	29	30	19	14	5	2

The Multivariate Analysis of Borrowing

The cross-tabulations reported above cannot tell the whole story since graduates differ along many dimensions other than gender and field of study, and these differences may affect borrowing. In order to analyze the independent effects of other variables on the probability of borrowing, we estimated multivariate regression models (see Appendix C for tabulations of the results for bachelor's graduates).

Gender and Field of Study Patterns. We began by looking again at patterns by gender and field of study, holding constant many of the other factors that influence borrowing. The first multivariate finding of interest is that the determinants of borrowing were statistically different for men and women. We therefore estimated separate models by sex. This differentiation contrasts with the impression created by Tables 2 and 3, where the borrowing patterns of men and women seemed broadly similar. That similarity is, however, the result of offsetting differences in the structure of borrowing and average characteristics that happened to leave men and women at similar overall borrowing levels. That is, the overall means mask some important underlying differences.

The regression results indicate that, holding other variables constant, male graduates were, in fact, *more* likely than females to have borrowed, especially in the first two cohorts. For the latest cohort, however, the male-female differences in predicted borrowing narrowed considerably. Furthermore, differences in the cumulative amount borrowed were considerably smaller than the differences in the probability of having borrowed.

The pattern of results across fields of study is also interesting. We found that, after controlling for other factors, certain fields were characterized by more borrowing than others. Some of these patterns held across all three cohorts of graduates. What is perhaps most interesting, however, is that those groups that borrowed the most were not generally those that had higher postgraduation earnings.

Specifically, the incidence of borrowing was generally lower among graduates with degrees in other social sciences (low average postgraduation incomes) and in commerce, economics, and law, other medical and health, and mathematics and physical sciences (all high-income fields). The tendency to borrow was somewhat greater for those in fine arts and humanities and in agricultural and biological sciences (both low-income fields) and in engineering (a high-income field). The highest rates of borrowing were for graduates in education and medicine (both high-income fields). Average levels of borrowing yielded similarly diverse patterns.

These findings are inconsistent with the hypothesis that students with higher expected future earnings are more willing to borrow (on the grounds that they want to shift spending forward in time, given their anticipation of greater capacity to repay the larger amounts in the postgraduation years). Instead, the results support the idea that many students borrowed to the maximum permitted regardless of their expected incomes — that is, that borrowing was largely supply driven (driven by the eligibility rules that determine the amounts available for borrowing), not demand driven.

In summary, the gender and field patterns are interesting for several reasons. First, they provide a useful description of borrowing patterns along these two important dimensions while controlling for other factors. Second, it is useful to know that student borrowing does not appear to have been demand driven (that is, that those with higher expected future incomes did not generally tend to borrow more than those with lower incomes); rather, it seems to have been determined largely by the eligibility rules. Finally, the results suggested that the observed borrowing patterns would translate into different repayment burdens by gender and field (a hypothesis that is confirmed below).

Provincial Patterns. Our regression results revealed wide differences in borrowing by province, probably because of the differences in need-assessment procedures and in the mixes of provincial and federal support that characterized the Old CSLP and the companion provincial programs. Graduates from Atlantic Canada were consistently most likely to have borrowed, and Albertans typically ranked second. British Columbians had borrowing rates in the middle rank, while students from the other western provinces were less likely to be borrowers. Quebecers were near the average, but they had an upward trend across the cohorts, while Ontarians slipped from the middle range to the lowest group in the most recent cohort.

Many of these provincial effects were quantitatively large, as well as statistically significant. For example, in the 1990 cohort, a typical individual was more than twice as likely to have a student loan if he or she was from Atlantic Canada than from Ontario.

In terms of amounts borrowed, the provincial effects were somewhat more mixed and less strong (as measured either by the magnitude or statistical significance of the estimated coefficients). An interesting and recurring result, however, was that graduates from Atlantic Canada tended to borrow the most in dollar values (which goes with the finding that they were most likely to be borrowers). In contrast, average borrowing among Ontario graduates declined over time, so that by 1992, they (and Quebec graduates) had the lowest borrowing levels of all.

Other Patterns. Socioeconomic background, as proxied by parental education, produced surprisingly small differences in the analysis, suggesting that the Old CSLP was not particularly effective in delivering more financial assistance to those with greater need.[10]

Students who had moved away from their home province to attend school did more borrowing than those who remained in-province, especially in the most recent cohort.

None of the other independent variables produced a consistent pattern of coefficient estimates.

---

10 We note, however, that the NGS data are not ideally suited to addressing this question, since parental education is a limited measure of socioeconomic background.

A Profile of Borrowing
by Graduate Students

Table 2 suggested that master's students had less borrowing than bachelor's graduates, and PhD students (men, at any rate) the least of all. How could this be? The longitudinal nature of the NGS data provides a unique opportunity for addressing the question. To that end, Table 5 compares borrowing levels as of graduation at the bachelor's level for those members of the 1986 cohort[11] who went on to graduate school with that of those who stopped at the first degree. The numbers show that those who had obtained a master's degree by 1988 had a much lower incidence of borrowing at the bachelor's level (although the mean amounts were high for the few who had borrowed). There was a similar relationship for those who had obtained their master's by 1991 (the time of the second interview), although the difference was not as great. Thus, there were indeed substantial increases in borrowing as individuals (especially women) moved from the bachelor's level to the master's, but those who continue their studies tended to have lower levels of borrowing at the bachelor's level.[12]

Table 5 reveals a similar pattern for PhD students: the proportion of graduates with loans at the master's level was much lower for those who went to a doctoral program than for those who did not. (The pattern is less clear for those who began a PhD after 1988, but there were many fewer such individuals in the data base, so it is the first group that dominates the overall outcome.)

There are at least three reasons those who went on to higher degrees should have borrowed less than others at the earlier stages. First, continuing students are generally the better students, and they,

---

11 We used the 1986 cohort because it was the most recent one for which we had data from two interviews.

12 It does not matter that the initial average loan *levels* at the bachelor's level were higher for those who went on to a master's degree. The much lower proportion with loans means that a large number of the masters' graduates started their loan balances at zero when they entered graduate school. That is, those who went on to a master's degree had less borrowing at the bachelor's level.

Table 5:   ***Borrowing and Continued Education,***
1986 Graduates

Extent of Education	Gender	Incidence	Mean
		(%)	($)[a]
Bachelor's graduates			
Stopped at bachelor's[b]	Male	44	7,970
	Female	39	7,920
Received master's by 1988	Male	15	8,370
	Female	4	6,720
Received master's by 1991	Male	24	6,610
	Female	25	7,330
Master's graduates			
Stopped at master's[b]	Male	33	7,320
	Female	31	6,850
Received PhD by 1988	Male	3	9,380
	Female	3	6,790
Received PhD by 1991	Male	42	6,370
	Female	39	7,790

[a]   Constant 1990 dollars.

[b]   Individuals may have been enrolled in, but did not receive, a higher degree after graduation in 1986.

therefore, would have received more financial support in the form of bursaries and scholarships at the lower degree levels, thus reducing their demand and eligibility for loans. Second, individuals from families with high incomes (in our models, those whose parents had high levels of education) have less need for loans, are less likely to be eligible for loan programs, and are more likely to go on to graduate studies; the confluence of these factors generated a negative correlation between borrowing at the earlier degree levels and ultimate educational attainment. Third, the anticipation of high levels of accumulated debt may have deterred some individuals from continuing their studies.

In short, our findings indicate that, at least in the past, most graduate students did not accumulate huge debts. That said, some individuals did see their total borrowing mount to quite high levels as they continued their studies (Table 4), and the problem may be worse now than it was in the 1980s.

The Burden of Student Borrowing

How great a burden did this borrowing represent? To answer this question, we looked at debt-to-earnings ratios, defining them as the amount owed to SLPs as of graduation divided by the earnings in the job held at the first interview.[13] A higher debt-to-earnings ratio generally indicates a heavier effective debt burden; a lower ratio, a lighter burden.[14]

Gender and Degree Patterns. Average debt-to-earnings ratios are shown in Table 6 and Figure 5.[15] The first general result is that debt burdens

---

13 We included in this analysis only those who held a job as of the first interview. Although there would have been some advantage in using earnings in a job closer to graduation, the first interview is the earliest point for which earnings are available in the NGS files. Furthermore, one could argue that the two-years-after-graduation figures used here give a better representation of the long-run situation than figures from earlier jobs would.

   It should also be noted that for individuals in jobs expected to last less than the full year, the earnings figures were the respondent's estimate of what he or she would earn on an annual basis (not what was actually earned) and thus represent a rate of pay rather than actual income.

14 Debt-to-earnings ratios are, however, only a rough index of debt load. The true burden probably also depends on the level of income since a greater ratio may be easier to bear at a higher income level, where there is more disposable income. For example, repaying $1,000 in loans out of an income of $10,000 may be more difficult than repaying $10,000 from an income of $100,000. In addition, the debt considered should include all debt, not just student loan debt, but this information was not available to us.

15 The table shows *median* debt-to-earnings ratios (that is, half of the graduates have a ratio above this value, half below). In this case, medians are reasonable indicators than arithmetic means, in which extreme values can be distorting.

Table 6:   ***Debt-to-Earnings Ratios[a] (Median),*** ***1982, 1986, and 1990***

	Gender	1982	1986	1990
		(percent)		
College/CEGEP	Male	12	19	20
	Female	15	23	26
Bachelor's	Male	14	25	28
	Female	17	29	32
Master's	Male	13	18	19
	Female	15	17	24
PhD	Male	9	12	15
	Female	10	9	15

[a]   Defined as the amount owed to student loans programs at graduation divided by annual earnings in the job held as of the first interview.

Figure 5:   ***Debt-to-Earnings Ratios,*** ***1982, 1986, and 1990***

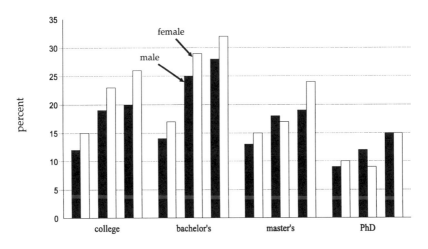

1st bar = 1982 cohort   2nd bar = 1986 cohort   3rd bar = 1990 cohort

Source: Table 6.

increased across the three cohorts for all gender/education groups, with the greatest increases for bachelor's graduates.

A second finding is that student debt burdens were uniformly higher for women than men, except at the PhD level. Not surprisingly, the similarities in borrowing levels by gender (Table 2) translated into unequal debt-to-earnings ratios because of women's lower earnings. Recall too that these figures are only for those who held jobs. Debt burdens are likely to be greater for nonworkers than for those with jobs, so the implications of the findings are strengthened by the fact that women's employment rates were lower than men's.[16]

A third point is that debt burdens among university graduates declined with degree, primarily because of the underlying differences in earnings levels (debt levels having already been seen to be similar.) College graduates' burdens were similar to those of master's graduates (and thus lower than those of bachelor's graduates.)

Field of Study Patterns. The more detailed view provided in Table 7 reveals that debt-to-earnings ratios for bachelor's graduates varied significantly by field of study. The pattern appears to be related to postgraduation income levels. For example, for men of the 1990 cohort, burdens ranged from a low of 21 percent for graduates in mathematics and physical sciences and engineering (high average income fields) to a high of 35 percent for those in agricultural and biological sciences (low-income fields). For women, they varied from a low of 25 percent for graduates in science and engineering (high-income fields) to a high of 38 percent for other social sciences (low-income fields).

Interestingly, the debt burdens were, in most cases, considerably more equal for men and women in a given field of study than for all bachelor's graduates taken together and were actually lower for women than men in certain fields. The implication is that women had

---

16 A point that feeds into our findings on repayment problems, reported in the next
   section.

Table 7:   *Debt-to-Earnings Ratios (Median) by Field, Bachelor's Graduates, 1982, 1986, and 1990*

Field of Study	Gender	1982	1986	1990
			(percent)	
Education	Male	18	28	34
	Female	19	31	34
Fine arts & humanities	Male	16	35	33
	Female	21	36	32
Commerce, economics, law	Male	13	27	30
	Female	18	28	32
Other social sciences	Male	15	31	32
	Female	19	37	38
Agriculture & biosciences	Male	12	27	31
	Female	21	27	31
Engineering	Male	12	20	21
	Female	*a*	11	25
Medical & health	Male	13	15	27
	Female	14	19	29
Maths & physical sciences	Male	15	20	21
	Female	19	23	25

[a]   Too few observations to be reported.

the higher overall debt burden more because they were concentrated in low-income fields than because they had lower earnings than men within a given field. Thus, to the degree that field of study is a choice, so too was a sizable proportion of women's higher debt loads.

Dispersion. The distribution of graduates over different ranges of debt-to-earnings ratios (not shown here) reveals a wide dispersion of debt loads. This point is relevant to the evaluation and comparison of loan systems: looking only at the average situation is far from enough because the plan must work well for the wide range of situations that exists in the population.

The Rate of Repayment
of Student Loans

We analyzed loan repayment rates by inspecting the proportion of the loan paid back by the first interview, two years after graduation.[17] The data in Table 8, also represented in Figure 6, show that the 1990 cohort of college and bachelor's students had, on average, repaid approximately half of their loans two years after graduation; that repayment rates were a little higher for the master's group; and that PhD graduates had repaid the highest proportion of all (about three-fifths of the debt they held at graduation). In all cases, the graduates of 1990 had paid back slightly smaller proportions of their debts than those of 1986.

Table 9 presents the distribution of repayment rates for the 1990 cohort. At one end of the distribution are those who had repaid their loans in full within two years of graduation (the last column in the table): about one-quarter of all college and bachelor's graduates, one-third of the master's graduates, and two-fifths of the PhD graduates. At the other end of the repayment spectrum, 35 to 45 percent of the bachelor's and college graduates had repaid less than 30 percent of their debt (the first two columns taken together), with a little more than one-third of the master's graduates and a slightly lower proportion of the PhD students similarly encumbered.

We can focus on graduates for whom debt was likely to be more of a problem by looking at repayment rates only for those who still had outstanding loan balances two years after graduation (that is, excluding the 25 to 40 percent who had paid their debts off completely). The last two columns of Table 8 (see also Figure 6) show that repayment rates were substantially lower for this group, which had repaid only about one-third of all their borrowing after two years.

---

17 We can present results for the 1986 and 1990 cohorts only, since the NGS did not ascertain the debt outstanding at the first interview for the 1982 cohort.

Table 8: *Proportion of Debt Repaid (Mean)*
Two Years after Graduation, 1986 and 1990

	Gender	All Borrowers		Borrowers with Loan Balances Remaining	
		1986	1990	1986	1990
		(percent)			
College/CEGEP	Male	55	53	27	36
	Female	55	51	29	35
Bachelor's	Male	50	48	34	33
	Female	51	46	35	31
Master's	Male	58	53	37	33
	Female	62	56	37	34
PhD	Male	64	63	41	37
	Female	73	60	41	33

Figure 6: *Proportion of Debt Repaid Two Years*
after Graduation, 1986 and 1990

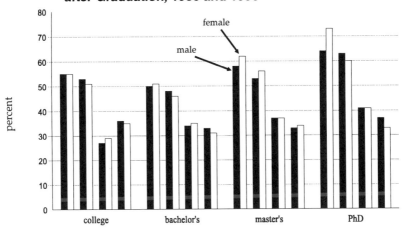

1st bar = 1986 cohort   2nd bar = 1990 cohort
3rd bar = 1986 cohort, only those with debt remaining
4th bar = 1990 cohort, only those with debt remaining

Source: Table 8.

Table 9:   Distribution of Debt Repayment, 1990 Graduates

	Gender	Less than 15%	15–30%	30–45%	45–60%	60–75%	75–100%	100%
					(percent)			
College/CEGEP	Male	14	22	16	13	6	5	25
	Female	16	23	18	9	5	5	24
Bachelor's	Male	15	26	18	10	5	4	23
	Female	17	27	17	10	4	3	22
Master's	Male	13	25	14	10	4	3	30
	Female	12	22	16	9	4	4	33
PhD	Male	11	18	11	9	5	5	41
	Female	8	25	10	11	5	1	40

Gender Patterns. Of greatest interest here is that the gender differences in repayment *rates* did not generally correspond to the gender differences in repayment *burden*. For example, in the case of 1990 college graduates, the median debt-to-earnings ratio (see Table 6) for women was 30 percent higher than the ratio for men, whereas the women's average payback rate was barely lower than the men's. A similar situation held for bachelor's graduates. For the master's group, the payback rates of women were actually higher than those of men, despite the former's greater debt loads.

In all three degree groups, women repaid their loans at similar or higher rates than men, even though their debts represented greater burdens in relation to their income levels.[18] This pattern broke at the PhD level, however, where women paid back at a slightly lower rate than men, despite having similar debt ratios.

Field of Study Patterns. Table 10 sets out the differences in payback rates by field of study for bachelor's graduates. In general, those with higher debt-to-earnings ratios tended to pay back lower proportions of their loans. These differences in repayment rates by field were, however, not as pronounced as the differences in debt burdens. This asymmetry was likely the result of the facts that borrowing tended to be similar across fields and that repayment schedules were largely independent of income.

In particular fields of study, as in the aggregate, women's generally higher debt-to-earnings ratios did not uniformly translate into lower payback rates. For example, the 1990 female engineering graduates had a higher average debt-to-earnings ratio than men but also a higher repayment rate. In other words, although student

---

18 The samples used to calculate the debt-to-earnings ratios and the payback rates were not identical. The debt-to-earnings calculations included only graduates with jobs, while the payback rates were calculated over all borrowers, regardless of the employment situation. This difference actually *reinforces* the male-female aspect of the findings; because men have higher employment rates, one would expect them to pay back an even higher proportion of their loans.

Table 10:   *Proportion of Debt Repaid (Mean) by Field,*
Bachelor's Graduates, 1986 and 1990

Field of Study	Gender	1986	1990
		(percent)	
Education	Male	46	44
	Female	50	43
Fine arts & humanities	Male	37	50
	Female	47	49
Commerce, economics, law	Male	46	45
	Female	47	44
Other social sciences	Male	47	52
	Female	55	41
Agriculture & biosciences	Male	60	48
	Female	56	52
Engineering	Male	61	53
	Female	55	57
Medical & health	Male	51	50
	Female	59	52
Maths & physical sciences	Male	52	51
	Female	53	50

borrowing appears to have been a greater burden for women, they repaid a greater portion of their loans in the two years following graduation. In other fields, however, debt ratios and payback rates corresponded more closely. Other social sciences are a good example in this regard: women had debt ratios considerably higher than men, and substantially lower repayment rates.

These results suggests the interesting — and potentially important — hypothesis that women may be both more cautious with their borrowing and more determined in their repayment. Further evidence, however, is required to test this notion more completely.

The Multivariate Analysis
of Repayment Rates

Our regression analysis (see Appendix C) gives a more detailed view of repayment rates.[19] Looking at repayment rates by gender while taking other factors into account offers evidence that women with a given set of characteristics tended to repay their loans more quickly than similar men in one cohort but not the other.

Field of Study Patterns. As for differences by field of study, the regressions show that, after controlling for other variables (including current earnings and amount owed at graduation), the estimated coefficients on the field of study variables remained statistically significant and sometimes quantitatively quite large. For example, in the 1990 cohort, the proportion repaid by women with engineering degrees was 50 percent higher than for women in the other social sciences group. Yet there was no obvious general pattern in terms of average incomes and repayment rates. For example, the low-income graduates in fine arts and humanities had below-average payback rates — as might be expected — but the higher-earning graduates from education and commerce, economics, and law were also among those who paid back at the lowest rates.

As for the relationships between repayment rates, the amount borrowed, and annual earnings, these variables had the expected signs, were statistically significant, and in some cases represented relatively large effects. The greater the borrowing or the lower the postgraduation earnings, the less the proportion repaid. Furthermore, putting the effects of income and amount borrowed together with the effects associated with field of study resulted in some substantial differences in predicted payback rates. To give an ex-

---

19 These findings are based on the estimation of double-censored tobit models of the proportion repaid between graduation and the first NGS interview two years later. These econometric models are the appropriate ones because they take into account the fact that there are two technical censoring points: the individual can pay back no less than zero and no more than the complete loan.

treme example, women who graduated in 1990 with a degree in mathematics and physical sciences (the highest rate of repayment) and had $4,000 less in loans and $10,000 more in earnings had a predicted repayment rate of approximately 67 percent; in comparison, the lower-earning, more indebted graduates in other social sciences (the lowest rate of repayment) had a rate of only 43 percent.

Other Patterns. Of the other variables in the repayment models, province turned out to be an important factor, even after controlling for field of study, the amount borrowed, annual earnings, and the other factors represented in the models. In general, the results correspond to provincial income patterns: graduates from Atlantic Canada and Quebec (low-income provinces) repaid at the slowest rates; those from Ontario, Alberta, and British Columbia (high-income provinces) paid back the fastest; graduates from the other western provinces lay in the middle. These effects were sometimes large. For example, for the 1990 female graduates, the coefficient estimates indicate a difference of 40 percentage points, on average, in the expected payback rates of a Quebec graduate and one of similar characteristics living in Saskatchewan.

Having moved to go to school was associated with slower payback, and part-time studies with speedier repayment. The other variables included in the models generated rather mixed results except for the presence of children, which was associated with lower repayment rates in every case.

Difficulties with Repayment

The NGS surveys of the 1986 and 1990 cohorts asked those who still owed money two years after graduation if they had experienced difficulties in repaying their student loans.[20] Between 20 and 30 percent said yes (see Table 11 and Figure 7).

20 That the data report self-identified repayment difficulties presents a potential problem: two individuals in similar situations may have described their experiences differently. But there is no obvious reason the distribution of responses...

A little arithmetic lets us put the incidence of repayment problems in a useful overall context. Of the three cohorts of graduates treated in our analysis, more than half had finished their studies free of government loans (Table 2) and thus faced no repayment burden at all. Furthermore, some 25 to 40 percent of those who did borrow had fully repaid their loans within two years of graduation (Table 9), well ahead of schedule and thus may be presumed not to have been overly burdened by their loans. Combining those two proportions with the 70 to 80 percent who did not report repayment difficulties (Table 11), we infer that only 7 to 8 percent of all postsecondary graduates experienced difficulties with the repayment of student loans.

That statement requires some caveats, however. First, our research looked only at graduates, and one expects that those who incurred loans but did not complete their programs may have been prime candidates for repayment problems. Furthermore, some of those who repaid their loans rapidly may have done so only with difficulty. Finally, as previously discussed, the most recent graduates covered by our data are those of 1990; it is virtually certain that the financial situation of graduates has become generally more difficult since that time and, therefore, that repayment problems have become more widespread.

Sector and Degree Patterns. A closer analysis of Table 11 suggests that women had a greater incidence of repayment problems than men. There were, however, exceptions: among 1986 PhD graduates and 1990 college graduates, women reported a lower incidence of prob-

---

Note 20 - cont'd.

...should differ between one group of graduates and another (for example, between men and women), so the measure should at least be an index of repayment problems.

The measure could be especially useful for evaluating alternative loan systems. Students who experienced repayment difficulties under the Old CSLP should be among those who could benefit most from the greater flexibility of the income contingent repayment (ICR) systems described below but would probably also be hit hardest by any tuition increases.

Table 11:   *Incidence of Difficulty in Repaying Loans,[a] 1986 and 1990*

	Gender	1986	1990	
		SLP or Non-SLP[b]	SLP or Non-SLP[b]	SLP Only
		(percent)		
College/CEGEP	Male	19	27	25
	Female	22	25	23
Bachelor's	Male	26	21	19
	Female	30	25	23
Master's	Male	20	22	20
	Female	26	26	23
PhD	Male	28	28	18
	Female	21	29	23

[a] Calculated for those with student debt still outstanding at the first interview, two years after graduation.

[b] Constructed to indicate difficulties in repaying either government (SLP) or other (non-SLP) student loans (see footnote 35 in the text).

Figure 7:   *Incidence of Difficulty in Repaying Loans, 1986 and 1990*

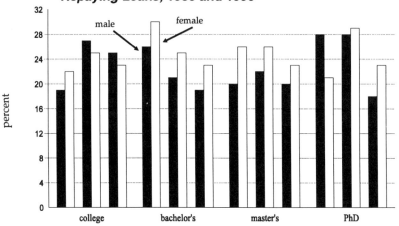

1st bar = 1986 cohort, SLP or non-SLP   2nd bar = 1990 cohort, SLP or non-SLP
3rd bar = 1990 cohort, SLP only

Source: Table 11.

lems than men. When one compares the 1986 and 1990 cohorts, the data show that repayment difficulties increased for college graduates and for female PhD graduates, decreased for bachelor's graduates, and changed little for master's graduates and PhD men.[21] Finally, the incidence of repayment problems was roughly similar for 1990 graduates across the various university degree levels; given the lower debt burdens at the advanced levels, this result is somewhat surprising. College graduates had a slightly greater rate of reported difficulties with government loans than did the bachelor's graduates.

Given the differences in debt-to-earnings ratios by field of study seen above (Table 7), one might expect similar variations in the proportion of graduates with repayment problems. This was indeed the case. Table 12 reports the results for bachelor's graduates. Their incidence of repayment problems with government loans was as high as 37 percent for female fine arts and humanities graduates of 1990 and as low as 8 percent for male and female medicine and health graduates of the same cohort.

Reasons for Difficulties. What were the underlying causes of difficulties in repaying loans? This question was asked of the 1986 graduates (but not the 1990 cohort) who still had debt outstanding as of the first interview. The results are shown in Table 13. Despite the ambiguity that comes from the overlapping categories and the multiple responses permitted, it is clear that the main problems were unemploy-

---

21 Comparing results across the two cohorts presents some problems. The variable for the earlier cohort was based on a single question regarding difficulties with *any* type of student loan, whereas the survey of the 1990 cohort posed two separate questions (with different skip patterns in the questionnaire) regarding government versus nongovernment loans. In an attempt to render the figures across the two cohorts more comparable, we constructed a single composite variable for the 1990 graduates, which we used along with one reflecting difficulties with government loans in particular. Ancillary analysis suggests, however, that these data differences probably have a fairly small effect on the 1986/90 comparisons.

Table 12:   ***Repayment Difficulties by Field,***
                Bachelor's Graduates,[a] 1986 and 1990

Field of Study	Gender	1986 SLP or Non-SLP[b]	1990 SLP or Non-SLP[b]	SLP Only
		(percent)		
Education	Male	24	17	16
	Female	29	24	22
Fine arts & humanities	Male	47	30	31
	Female	40	40	37
Commerce, economics, law	Male	23	18	17
	Female	28	19	18
Other social sciences	Male	38	26	23
	Female	42	29	28
Agriculture & biosciences	Male	11	26	23
	Female	16	28	29
Engineering	Male	15	20	17
	Female	23	27	19
Medical & health	Male	13	12	8
	Female	15	13	8
Maths & physical sciences	Male	27	19	16
	Female	8	15	16

[a] Calculated for those with student debt still outstanding at the first interview, two years after graduation.

[b] Constructed to indicate difficulties in repaying either government (SLP) or other (non-SLP) student loans (see Chapter 3, fn 21).

ment and insufficient earnings, not high debt load (except for PhD men) or other reasons.

A possible explanation of these findings is that certain graduates may have had unreasonable expectations regarding their early career opportunities, taken on too much debt, and then blamed their employment situation for their difficulties with loan repayment, even though the fundamental problem was that they simply had not

Table 13:   *Reasons for Difficulties in Repaying Loans, 1986 Graduates*

	Gender	Un-employed	Insufficient Earnings	High Debt Load	Other Reasons
		(percent)			
College/CEGEP	Male	37	53	15	10
	Female	32	50	15	13
Bachelor's	Male	32	54	21	13
	Female	34	50	13	15
Master's	Male	36	47	17	11
	Female	34	46	21	11
PhD	Male	25	28	38	13
	Female	*a*	*a*	*a*	*a*

a   Too few observations to be reported.

Note: Data for those with student debt (government or otherwise) still outstanding at the first interview, two years after graduation. The rows sum to more than 100 percent because individuals could indicate multiple causes.

been aware of the job market outcomes they could expect. On the other hand, changed labor market conditions may have rendered initially rational choices less remunerative. Finally, certain individuals may simply have encountered bad luck.

A more direct view of the relationship between loan problems and labor market status is presented in Table 14. Of the borrowers with loans still outstanding two years after graduation, about 20 percent reported difficulties with repayment. Presuming that those who had already fully repaid their loans (some 25 percent) had experienced no difficulties, the percentage of all borrowers with full-time jobs who had repayment problems was quite small — some 10 to 15 percent. But repayment difficulties were much more widespread for those working part time, unemployed, or not in the labor force.

Finally, it is interesting to look at repayment problems by income level, as shown in Table 15 for bachelor's graduates.[22] Not

---

22 Our calculations include only those with jobs as of the first interview.

Table 14:   *Incidence of Repayment Difficulties,*
              by Current Labor Force Status, 1990 Graduates

	Gender	Working Full Time	Working Part Time	Un-employed	Not in Labor Force
			(percent)		
College/CEGEP	Male	20	47	46	*a*
	Female	18	34	36	47
Bachelor's	Male	17	22	35	*a*
	Female	20	26	40	33
Master's	Male	14	37	57	a
	Female	20	30	30	34
PhD	Male	14	*a*	*a*	*a*
	Female	20	*a*	*a*	*a*

a Too few observations to be reported.

surprisingly, repayment problems generally decreased at higher income levels. What is more interesting is that there are fairly clear-cut points beyond which each gender/education group had markedly fewer problems. That this phenomenon is especially true for men makes sense, since variations in women's incomes are more likely to reflect family-related labor supply decisions.

The Multivariate Analysis
of Difficulty with Repayment

In the cross-tabulations, women seemed more likely to report difficulties than men in both the 1986 and 1990 cohorts. For the 1990 cohort, the results of our multivariate analysis (see Appendix C) confirmed that female graduates reported more problems than men even when we held other variables statistically constant. These gender patterns did not hold for the 1986 cohort, however, in which we found a tendency for women to report fewer problems for a given set of characteristics.

Table 15:   *Incidence of Repayment Difficulties,*
by Income Class, Bachelor's Graduates,
1986 and 1990

Gender	Income[a]	1986	1990
		(percent)	
Male	Less than $15,000	55	37
	$15,000 to $19,999	41	42
	$20,000 to $24,999	17	22
	$25,000 to $29,999	16	15
	$30,000 to $34,999	10	15
	$35,000 or more	6	15
	Unknown or not stated	*b*	17
Female	Less than $15,000	46	44
	$15,000 to $19,999	39	35
	$20,000 to $24,999	18	28
	$25,000 to $29,999	14	24
	$30,000 to $34,999	12	14
	$35,000 or more	7	14
	Unknown or not stated	*b*	32

[a]   Constant 1990 dollars.

[b]   Too few observations to be reported.

The results by field of study were generally consistent with the cross-tabulations in that low-income fields were characterized by a significantly higher incidence of repayment problems in both cohorts, even after controlling for other factors. Furthermore, the differences by field were quantitatively important, with certain fields having pre-dicted probabilities of repayment problems several times larger than those of others.

The multivariate results also showed that the amount borrowed and the individual's earnings had the expected effects on repayment difficulties and were quantitatively important in most cases.[23] The earnings effect was particularly strong for women, especially in the 1990 cohort, where it was almost ten times as strong as it was for men. Evidently, higher earnings reduced the probability of having difficulty much more for women than for men. In short, the graduate's gender, field of study, amount borrowed, and level of earnings proved strong determinants of repayment problems — results that were predicted but are nevertheless interesting in the magnitudes of the effects. Furthermore, the gender differences in the income effects were unanticipated and are therefore of special interest.

The differences by province were again generally statistically significant and often large, but they followed no clear pattern. The results for the array of variables representing schooling characteristics were mixed; in only a few cases did these variables enter all models with the same sign and significance. Parental education also generated mixed findings across the four gender-cohort models.

Having moved to attend school was an exception, with movers experiencing a higher incidence of repayment problems than non-movers. Age was positively associated with repayment problems, being married implied fewer problems, and the presence of children increased the risk of difficulties.

---

23 For example, an extra $1,000 in loans increased the probability of repayment problems by 1 to 7 percent across the four models, while an extra $5,000 in earnings reduced the risk by 2 to 17 percent.

Chapter 4

The New CSLP

The most recent data used in the statistical analysis presented in the previous chapter are from 1992, for students who graduated in 1990. Since then, there have been many changes in the educational experiences of postsecondary graduates and in the world they face at graduation. Moreover, the Canada Student Loans Program (CSLP) itself has changed substantially, especially since the legislative reforms enacted in 1994.[1] The important differences between the Old CSLP and the New CSLP are summarized in Table 16. In this chapter, we offer our best guesses about the efficacy of four major changes.

Increased Loan Limits

One of the most heralded changes of the CSLP has been the substantial increases in borrowing limits: from $105 to $165 per week of school for full-time students. Lending limits had been frozen for ten years, so these increases were long overdue — especially given the sharp tuition rises of the early 1990s.

The question remains, however, as to the adequacy of these new limits, especially for students with limited access to other sources of financing. The CSLP has, of course, never been intended to provide the amounts required to meet all the expenses associated with postsecondary studies.[2] Nevertheless, still-higher borrowing limits, in one form or another, might well be appropriate.

---

1 Many loans made under the Old CSLP are of course, still outstanding. For them, the old rules continue.

2 In addition, grant programs are in place to take into account the special circumstances of some categories of students who face particular hardship (see Table 16).

Table 16: Comparison of the "Old" and "New" Canada Student Loans Programs

Item	"Old" CSLP	"New" CSLP
Mission	• help needy students access postsecondary education	• help needy students access postsecondary education; • encourage successful, timely completion of studies
Eligibility criteria	• full time, defined as 60% of full course load; • any combination of courses allowed; • scholastic standards left to institution to define and monitor; • limit of 520 weeks (15 academic years) on total borrowing, with discretion to limit borrowing by level of study; • reinstatement based on efforts to repay over 12-month period or circumstances beyond borrower's control	• full time, defined as 60% of full course load; • program must lead to degree, diploma, or certificate • satisfactory progress defined as successful completion of 60% of full course load; • lifetime borrowing limit of 340 weeks (400 for PhD studies, 520 for students with disabilities) • assistance limited to normal program length plus one additional period of studies • reinstatement based on rehabilitation agreement with lender (borrower pays interest and up to six consecutive payments
Needs assessment	• complex procedures, with great variation among provinces	• standardized approach based on objective national databases with regional variations in cost
Meeting the need	• percentage of assistance met by federal government varied significantly among provinces	• 60% of full-time student's assessed need provided, up to federal government's weekly loan limit
Loan limits	• full-time weekly loan limit of $105; • maximum part-time loan balance of $2,500	• full-time weekly loan limit of $165; • maximum part-time loan balance of $4,000

Interest relief	• based on unemployment or temporary disability; • available for up to 18 months during 9½ years of repayment	• based on low income; • available for up to 18 months during first 5 years of repayment
Students with disabilities	• inadequate recognition of special costs; • forgiveness provision based on financial hardship	• annual special opportunity grants of up to $3,000; • forgiveness provision retained for students who become disabled prior to, or during, studies; • flexible eligibility requirements (for example, course load, weeks of borrowing)
Part-time students	• required to begin paying interest and principal on loans 30 days after receiving them; • no grant assistance	• during studies, required to pay only interest; begin to pay interest and principal 6 months after studies; • annual special opportunity grants of $1,200 for those with high needs
Women in certain PhD programs	• no special assistance	• special opportunity grants of up to $3,000 for up to 3 years
Loan forgiveness	• no forgiveness beyond death and disability provision	• proposed partial loan forgiveness to reduce debt load of neediest students
Student debt-management strategy	• limited attention to debt-load issues	• four-phase strategy being introduced

Table 16 - continued

Item	"Old" CSLP	"New" CSLP
Financing arrangements	• access for all eligible students with demonstrated financial need;	• access for all eligible students with demonstrated financial need;
	• full interest subsidy during full-time studies and for 6 months after;	• full interest subsidy during full-time studies; interest payments deferred for 6 months after studies;
	• 100% guarantee on loans;	• lender risk sharing based on contracts with nine participating lenders (5% risk premium; putback);
	• during studies, government paid lender annual interest based on Government of Canada one-to-five-year bond yields	• government pays lender interest at prime rate during studies
	• borrower paid lender fixed interest based on Government of Canada five-to-ten-year bond yields at consolidation;	• borrower pays interest at fixed (prime plus 5%) or floating (prime plus 2.5%) rate;
	• maximum repayment period of 9½ years	• repayment period to be negotiated between borrower and lender; no maximum
Arrangements with provinces	• no formal agreement with participating provinces;	• formal arrangements with participating provinces being developed (for example, policy and procedures manual, awards policy, disbursement policy, verification and audit, automated systems);
	• provinces that opted out received alternative payments based on program costs in participating provinces	• provinces that opt out will receive alternative payments based on program costs in participating provinces

Source: Canada 1996b.

Standardized Need-Assessment Procedures

One of the principal criticisms of the Old CSLP was provincial variation in the need-assessment procedures, which led to significant differences in eligibility depending on where the student was making his or her application. To address this problem, the CSLP commissioned a study of the existing provincial need-assessment procedures (Bennecon 1991) and convened a federal-provincial working group to come up with proposals.

The new *Policy and Procedures Manual* (Canada 1994a) contains a detailed reworking and most important, *standardization* of the eligibility criteria.[3] The policymakers hoped that if the provinces adopted the new procedures, a general tightening of need assessment and greater horizontal equity would result. The response from the provinces was quite positive. All except Ontario had adopted new procedures by the 1996/97 academic year.

The New CSLP should, therefore, result in more similar treatment for students across the country.[4] This is a significant step forward, as it should create a system that is substantially more fair both across individuals and in how the provinces themselves benefit from the CSLP. For example, whereas provinces could previously manipulate their own packages of financial aid to take maximum advantage of the CSLP money available, the new system restricts their room to maneuver by limiting CSLP loans to a maximum of 60 percent of assessed need (up to the weekly loan limits); the provinces then decide if and how to fund the remaining 40 percent.

It is not yet clear, however, if the changes will result in better-targeted student loans that deliver the aid where it is truly needed while limiting assistance to those with the resources to pay for their own postsecondary schooling.

---

3 For example, the treatment of parental incomes has been standardized, and educational expenses are to be based on Statistics Canada's regional price indexes, rather than on a single index for Toronto as under the old system.

4 Excepting Quebec and the Northwest Territories, which will continue to run their own programs with their own need-assessment procedures.

Shifting the
Responsibility for Collection

Probably the greatest criticism of the Old CSLP concerned default rates, which many observers believed were too high, at least partly because of aspects of the loan program itself. In response, the CSLP began a long series of negotiations with the banking industry aimed at shifting some of the default risk from the government to lenders.

Under the terms of the resulting contract, which was announced in August 1995 and will be in place for a period of five years, the financial structure of the CSLP is substantially changed, leaving it unlike any other student loan system in the world. The lending institutions are assuming the risk of default in return for a payment of 5 percent of the value of the loans that go into repayment each year. Aside from this risk premium, government expenditures on new loans will be limited to subsidizing the interest while students are in school plus paying for the interest relief program described later.[5] The government does, however, retain its critical role in determining loan eligibility and certain other aspects of student lending.

The working of this hybrid public-private plan and its likely consequences are worth considering in a little more detail. In many ways, students are unlikely to notice much difference from the old system. They continue to apply for loans through the appropriate provincial offices, which continue to carry out need-assessment procedures. As before, once eligibility for financial assistance has

---

5 There is also a "putback" option whereby the lender may, after having exhausted all reasonable means of collection, return up to 3 percent of its nonperforming loans to the government each year. The government will pay 5 percent of the face value of these debts (principal and interest) to the lender and then attempt to collect on those loans. Up to the 5 percent already paid out to the lender, collections will be retained by the government, while all further collection will be shared, with 25 percent retained by the government and 75 percent going to the lender.

  The precise collection mechanisms the government will use have not been fully specified at time of writing, but it is anticipated that setoffs against income tax returns will be one tool. the key point is that the putback provision appears to represent a limited form of bad debt relief for lenders and still leaves them with strong incentives to collect on all loans.

been established, a student can take out a loan at one of the participating financial institutions, which cannot refuse to grant it because
of their own assessment of the creditworthiness of the borrower.[6]
Furthermore, while the student is in school, the government will
continue to pay the interest on the loan. Thus, up to the point of
school leaving, the new system closely resembles the old.

At that time, however, it will be up to the student and the bank
to agree to repayment terms. Although the old ten-year schedule
remains an option, other arrangements are possible. In principle, the
banks should be receptive to working out a repayment schedule that
best suits an individual's particular circumstances. They may also
prove flexible in the face of changes in the situation, willing to reopen
negotiations and adjust the schedule as necessary. In addition, a
student will have more choice of interest rate strategies, since he or
she may now opt to let the loan rate float or stick to the fixed rates
that characterized the old system.

If repayment problems do emerge, the financial institution will
be wholly responsible for the collection of the loans. It can no longer
simply declare them in default and turn them over to the government for reimbursement of principal and interest. The government's
default-related costs will be a flat 5 percent of the value of loans going
into repayment, regardless of the actual loan-loss rate.

Certain other aspects of CSLP loans remain as before. For
example, they will continue to bear preferential interest rates determined by calculations based on the prime rates (see Table 16). This
feature will work to reduce loan losses by reducing the costs of loans
and leaving students better able to meet their repayment schedules
relative to what would be the case were interest rates set at (generally
higher) open market rates. On the down side, however, the lower-
than-market interest rates make student loans less profitable than
other assets in banks' portfolios, and may thus limit their willingness

---

6 The auditor-general notes (Canada 1990) that a relatively small number of
  students from private trade and vocational schools who were eligible for CSLP
  loans were responsible for a disproportionate share of defaults. Under the new
  agreement with the banks, the CSLP will study this problem.

to manage their student loans on a personalized basis. Furthermore, the relatively small size of student loans will continue to limit the banks' incentives to be as responsive as students might wish.

In short, the greater flexibility of repayment terms that former students desire ultimately will depend on the tradeoff between the increased incentives to collect on the loans and the continuing disincentives related to the smallness of and relatively low returns to student loans. Furthermore, the banks' willingness to be flexible may vary case by case — perhaps in ways related to individuals' attractiveness as banking customers.

Overall, shifting the responsibility for the collection of student loans to the banks should lead to some increased flexibility of repayment terms and a reduction in loan-loss rates, but the extent of these changes is difficult to predict. That said, in accepting full liability for the student loans portfolio in return for a 5 percent risk premium, the banks have implicitly indicated that they believe they can reduce default rates from previous levels — a clear improvement over the Old CSLP.

Changes in
Interest Rate Subsidies

The six-month postschooling grace period that had existed from the beginning of the CSLP was dropped for all loans negotiated after July 31, 1994. Students are now responsible for the interest on their loans from the time they leave school. At the same time, the interest relief program, which had been restricted to the unemployed and those who could not work because of temporary disability or illness, has now been extended to those in jobs with low earnings. As before, individuals can apply for assistance for periods of three months at a time and are eligible for a total of 18 months of aid. Now, however, interest relief is available only in the first five years of repayment. The government continues to assume responsibility for loans to those who die during studies or who are disabled and cannot make their repayments without undue hardship.

These changes seem to be in the right direction. Those who have the means to meet the costs of their loans from the time they leave school should do so, while it is quite reasonable to provide assistance to various categories of individuals facing financial difficulties as they make the transition from school to work. Furthermore, any calculation of the full benefits of the interest relief program should take into account the peace of mind all borrowers receive from knowing that, if they encounter difficulties in their early years in the job market, they will receive some assistance with their student loan.

The program is not particularly expensive. Expenditures on interest relief are expected to be just $46.5 million in 1996/97 (Canada 1996a, 2-72), although this estimate is roughly three times longer than previous levels.

Chapter 5

Income Contingent Repayment Loan Schemes

Of the various proposals for further improvement of the Canada Student Loans Program (CSLP), one frequently heard is the introduction of an income contingent repayment (ICR) scheme.

ICR programs can take a variety of forms, but there is one cardinal defining characteristic: the rate of repayment depends on the individual's income in the postschooling period. That is, instead of paying a fixed amount per month or year (as under the Old CSLP), a borrower pays a set percentage of his or her income — unless the individual's (or household's) income is below a chosen cutoff point, in which case no payment is required until circumstances improve. In the classic model, repayment is integrated with the income tax system in order to ensure payment and tokeep administrative costs down.

Although the idea of ICR student loans has been around since the 1940s, it has only recently received widespread attention in Canada. This surge of interest probably has several causes. First, ICR programs are now in place in Australia, New Zealand, the United Kingdom, Sweden, and the United States, setting some interesting examples that Canada might choose to follow. Second, Lloyd Axworthy's 1994 green paper on social policy (Canada 1994b) included the introduction of ICR as a central element, catapulting the issue into the public eye. Finally, the deepening fiscal crisis of the postsecondary system and the resulting tuition increases seem to have created a climate in which people see radical change as desirable —

and, in any event, inevitable — and are thus open to considering a new way of delivering financial assistance to students.[1]

The Many Faces of ICR

ICR loan systems can come in many different forms. Indeed, one of the confusions in the ICR debate is that different individuals sometimes assume that their understanding of ICR *is* ICR when they are actually discussing versions that do not correspond. For example, some people see ICR as a sort of general "graduate tax" that involves subsidies from high-earnings graduates to low-earnings graduates, while others imagine something that more closely resembles a traditional loan program, in which individuals choose to participate and simply repay the amounts they themselves have borrowed, with no built-in transfers from one group of graduates to another.

To help clarify the ICR debate, we begin by describing the different elements that can be involved.

Subsidies

In principle, an ICR loan system could be either entirely unsubsidized or subsidized so that borrowers repaid less than the full principal and interest. In an unsubsidized system, interest would begin to accrue as soon as the loan was issued, and interest rates would have to be high enough to cover any aggregate shortfall in repayment. A subsidized system could include interest payments while the individual was in school, preferential interest rates during

---

1 The classic reference here is Friedman (1955). See also Kruger and Bowen (1993). The ICR idea was supported in the mid-1980s by the Macdonald Commission (Canada 1985), Ontario's Bovey Commission (1984), and the 1991 report prepared for the Department of the Secretary of State (Bennecon 1991). On a more individual level, David Stager (see Stager and Derkach 1992) of the University of Toronto has been a long-standing advocate of ICR. For further discussion of the ebb and flow of the ICR idea in Canada, see AUCC (1993), Kesselman (1993), and West (1993).

the repayment period, and various forms of assistance during periods when earnings are low.

Another possible feature is the forgiveness of any balance still owing after a certain period of time — say, 20 years. Such a system could be self-financing (that is, operate without government subsidies) if those with higher earnings paid a higher interest rate or otherwise repaid somewhat more than the full value of what they borrowed, with the proceeds of those extra payments covering the losses sustained on those loans not paid off within the maximum repayment period.

Participation in an unsubsidized program would almost surely have to be mandatory. If it were not, those who expected to have higher earnings and, therefore, to pay back more than the amortized value of what they borrowed would tend to avoid the program and look for financing elsewhere. This adverse selection would undermine the solvency of the whole system. For this reason, at least some degree of subsidy would be almost unavoidable.

Any acceptance of the need for subsidies has further implications, however, particularly regarding limits on borrowing. Some ICR proponents advocate allowing students to borrow virtually whatever amounts they wish (within certain broad limits). Such a system would allow individuals to "bet" on their own futures, could be administratively simpler (it would have fewer eligibility rules to administer), and would provide whatever funds were necessary for postsecondary education. But if such an open-ended system had any significant degree of subsidy, it would end up providing subsidies to many students not really in need and could thus become very expensive. Hence, once subsidies were introduced, loans would probably have to be restricted.

Repayment Rates

Under an ICR system, repayment could be at either a constant or a varying percentage of income. In the latter case, the percentage would presumably rise with income and, therefore, ability to pay.

Furthermore, proposals often include a cutoff income level (for example, two-thirds of the average industrial earnings) below which an individual would pay nothing.

The definitions of income on which payments could be based are various. The ability to pay could, for example, be assessed by taking spousal income (and perhaps family circumstances) into account or not. Presumably, such decisions would be based on judgments of who is ultimately responsible for a student loan (does the responsibility become shared when one becomes married?), equity considerations (would restricting ability to pay to an individual basis result in reduced payments from a substantial number of individuals with wealthy spouses?), and the behavioral responses that could result from one treatment versus another (what might the effects be on labor supply?).

Policymakers would also have to decide matters such as which payroll deductions, if any, were to be taken into account when determining payments (contributions to pension plans?). Finally, the program would have to establish the precise income level below which no payment was required. A small — even token — contribution might be required of all borrowers, if only to help maintain contact between the collection system and the individual.

Loan Limits

As noted above, any subsidized ICR system would probably require setting limits on the maximum amount that could be borrowed. These limits would normally be based on the usual costs of a post-secondary education, perhaps restricted to tuition, fees, and other direct costs or expanded to include living expenses. The limits would presumably be determined in accord with the general purpose of the system — as a supplement to a more traditional loan system (which would imply a more limited set of admissible costs for the ICR component) or as a stand-alone program (thus implying broader limits).

The Arguments for ICR

Proponents of ICR present a variety of arguments for the program they favor. The preceding discussion should have made it apparent, however, that the different forms ICR systems can take mean that some of the advantages are relevant only to certain types. In what follows, we attempt to be clear about which kind of ICR carries the potential advantage being discussed.

Insurance against Default or Excessive Debt Burden

The greatest advantage claimed for ICR is the protection it offers borrowers by gearing payments to current income levels, providing other forms of assistance when earnings are low, and eventually forgiving the loans of those who have consistently low earnings after graduation. Thus, if tuition levels, the amount of subsidy in the system, borrowing limits, and so on were held constant, an ICR scheme should leave students unambiguously better off than a more rigid system such as the Old CSLP. However, if ICR were introduced at the same time as loan subsidy levels were reduced, tuition levels increased, or other changes introduced, the overall package might leave students worse off. In particular, their debt burdens might increase *despite* the introduction of ICR.

Provision of More Resources to Students

The primary goal of any postsecondary loan system is to provide access to funds for students, especially those from low-income families. By reducing the effective burden of a given level of borrowing (presuming subsidies were held constant), an ICR system should allow students to take on greater debt loads. Thus, it would represent a vehicle by which more funds were made available to help pay for their postsecondary studies.

Furthermore, to the degree that an ICR system cut the costs of the loan program (through lower default rates, reduced administration costs, and so on), loan limits could be increased or the savings otherwise returned to the system in the form of various enhancements (for example, expanded interest relief during periods of low earnings).

In short, an ICR plan (again, holding other factors constant) should generally provide increased financial resources for students who need funds for postsecondary schooling.

Lower Default Rates
and Administrative Costs

Other potential advantages of the ICR approach include the possible reduction of default rates and of various administrative costs. If, for instance, the loan system were run through the income tax system, as the classic ICR models advocate, lower collection costs and default rates should indeed result. These aspects are especially alluring in the face of current criticisms that some students abuse the loan system by reneging on payments they are perfectly capable of carrying, that the current system does not provide sufficient incentives for banks to collect on their student loans, and that the government has not been efficient in following up on defaulters. However, collection through the income tax system could, in principle, be implemented with a *non*-ICR system, meaning that these advantages should not be ascribed to ICR *per se*.

ICR is also often touted as a means of reducing the administrative burden of establishing loan eligibility. This advantage would, however, occur only in a system in which all students, regardless of their family income, could borrow as much as they wanted (up to the established limits), thus obviating the need for the eligibility tests. We have suggested, however, that such a system is unlikely to be adopted in practice; unlimited borrowing would almost certainly be permitted only with an unsubsidized system, and the selection problems it would entail would make enactment unlikely. In short, it is hard to imagine a system without some sort of means tests, so the administrative savings in this regard would be limited.

Summary of the Arguments for ICR

In our view, the principal advantage of the ICR approach *per se* is its tying of repayment to income. This flexibility would be especially attractive for younger people making the difficult transition from school to work. The addition of provisions for forgiving loans that had not been repaid within 20 or 25 years would provide additional insurance against chronically low earnings. Both of these features can be thought of as protection against the possibility of postsecondary education's not paying off for a individual financially.

The other advantages typically claimed for ICR systems are, however, either unlikely to be realized in practice or could probably be achieved with non-ICR systems as well. In short, one must carefully assess the advantages of the ICR approach in general and the characteristics of any particular system under consideration, comparing the benefits with what might be achieved with more traditional forms of loan systems.

The Arguments against ICR

Few people oppose the ICR idea of tying repayment to income or of reducing the effective burden of a given amount of borrowing and thus allowing students to borrow greater amounts of money. That said, ICR proposals often meet with substantial opposition, such as the largely hostile reception received by the 1994 Axworthy proposals (Canada 1994x). If ICR is so great, why is there so much opposition?

A Trojan Horse for Tuition Increases and Reduced Subsidies

Much of the opposition is focused not on the ICR approach itself but rather on other changes that typically have accompanied proposals for its introduction. Most important in this regard, many commentators seem to take a general anti-ICR position because they view the idea as a Trojan horse containing tuition increases or decreased loan subsidies (see, for example, Duncan 1992; 1993).

Short-Term Capital Requirements and Long-Term Financial Viability

Other analysts have substantial uncertainties about the true long-term costs of an ICR system. If it was operated by the government, as is generally advocated, the initial capital outlays could be substantial, given Treasury Board rules requiring that an amount equal to 25 percent of the money lent be budgeted to meet potential future losses. Although an ICR feature might, in fact, reduce default rates, the extent of this improvement is difficult to predict. The idea of provisions for eventually forgiving loans introduces further uncertainty because they would not be triggered for 20 or 25 years (when the first low-earning borrowers reached the end of the maximum repayment period). In short, moving to an ICR system would probably require substantial up-front capital costs and a variety of longer-term uncertainties, both of which would constitute significant disadvantages for the government.

Overly Long Repayment Periods

Tying repayment to income might imply that the repayment period for some borrowers would stretch out long past the standard ten-year period of the Old CSLP. For those individuals, the benefit of avoiding heavy monthly payments would likely come at the cost of paying out more money (because of accumulating interest) over a longer period of time. No doubt, many 40-year-olds would still be paying back their student loans.

To be sure, that situation would not necessarily be a bad thing, especially since an ICR system would, presumably, simply increase the range of choice in terms of repayment options, and individuals could always adopt the ten-year repayment term that characterized the Old CSLP.

Indirect Effects

Another area of uncertainty is the indirect effects of coupling an ICR scheme with the income tax system. In principle, loan payments would act as an additional tax on earnings. As such, they could adversely affect decisions regarding labor supply, family formation, participation in the informal economy, tax compliance, and other behavior.

Summary of the Arguments against ICR

In our view, the only major specific disadvantage of an ICR system is the uncertainties about its long-term financial viability — concerns arising from the uncertainty of default rates and from the possibility of adverse selection within an unsubsidized plan. The other objections seem to be either about non-ICR issues (such as higher tuition or lower subsidies) or speculative (repayment periods that are too long and indirect effects).

That said, many of the design issues just mentioned are far from trivial and would make the design and implementation of an ICR program very challenging.

Chapter 6

Conclusion

The Canada Student Loans Program (CSLP) has played an important role in improving the educational opportunities of postsecondary students, having issued loans to more than 2 million Canadians over its 30-odd years of existence. In light of the important recent changes in the program, we conclude by offering summary judgments of the New CSLP with some suggestions about how its performance might be judged in the years to come, several ideas for additional changes, and a broad view of postsecondary schooling in general.

The New CSLP: A Summary

The easiest way to summarize our judgment of the New CSLP is to comment on its new features.

Transferring Collection to the Banks

Will the transfer of collection responsibility to the financial institutions create a near-ICR program or a slippery slope leading to the inequitable treatment of students? To consider the question and its implications, one must return to basic principles.

The received wisdom is that government intervention is essential to the existence of a fair and efficient student loans system. Most students can offer very little collateral, and banks have difficulty in assessing the likelihood that the loans to them will be repaid. Thus, in theory, the private banking system would be reluctant to lend to students without government guarantees, resulting in a general underinvestment in student loans and reduced opportunities for postsecondary studies and the associated losses of private and social benefits. Furthermore, any loans made under a private system would tend go to the select group of students who represented good credit risks, principally those whose parents would be willing and able to provide guarantees — a serious equity problem. These arguments suggest that the government must step in with either direct lending or guarantees to private lenders. That is the rationale for the existence of the CSLP and similar systems in other countries.[1]

The new arrangement, whereby the banks are assuming full responsibility for the collection of student loans in return for a 5 percent risk premium while government retains control over the determination of eligibility and requires banks to lend to all who qualify, represents a new and interesting solution to the old student loans problem. We have already described how these changes should lead to lower default rates, reduced costs to the government, and greater flexibility in repayment schedules than under the old system — benefits that should result from shifting the responsibility for collection to the private sector, which is in the business of managing loan portfolios in the most efficient manner possible. Yet by retaining control over eligibility, the government can ensure that the equity aspects of the student loan system and the efficiencies of risk pooling are preserved. In short, the comparative advantages of the private sector in managing and collecting loans are being exploited while the broader goals of the student loan program are preserved by the government's control over lending.

At least, that is how it looks on paper. In practice, things may not work quite out so well. For example, students who seem more attractive as long-run clients may receive more favorable treatment than others, both when the loan is being taken out and, more important, during the repayment period when flexibility will be the relevant watchword. In particular, those whose parents or spouses are established clients and those with high earnings may receive preferential

---

1 See Mankiw (1986) for a discussion of these issues.

treatment. The size of the loan is also likely to be a factor. Thus, the risk of passing full management of collection over to the banks and opening up possibilities for efficiency and flexibility is that the door is similarly opened to inequitable treatment and favoritism.

We cannot predict how great this problem may be, but the government should be prepared. We offer two simple suggestions. First, the performance of the new system should be monitored along a number of dimensions, including the equity of treatment across student borrowers, especially with respect to differences by family income and graduates' own earnings. Second, the government should institute an appeal system for students who feel they are receiving unfair treatment, such as excessively rigid repayment regimes. (A system of mandatory arbitration would restrict appeals to those with merit.)

Getting the "Risk Premium" Right

Postsecondary students represent an attractive pool of customers for banks, which, therefore, generally wish to offer good service to *all* their student borrowers, thus enhancing their reputations and helping them build their client base. Indeed, it is useful to think of the banks' participation in the student loans system as having two distinct benefits.

The first is obviously the loan portfolio itself. The second is the access to a desirable client base. The full value of being in the student loan business consists, therefore, of the expected rate of return on the student loans *plus* the value of the future business that may be won by attracting student borrowers. Indeed, one would expect that banks would be willing to pay for the privilege of establishing a business relationship with such an attractive pool of clients (as they clearly do via the heavy advertising and other marketing strategies targeted on students and recent graduates).

This notion of the full value of student loans to the banks puts their recent negotiations with the government over the New CSLP in an interesting light. One should, for example, think of the premium the government pays the banks for student loans as compensation for their riskiness *offset* by the value of the student client base the banks gain by being in the student loan business. The greater the value of that client base, the more the offset of the risk premium. Indeed, at the limit, the net risk premium could even be negative — the banks might be willing to pay for the opportunity of making student loans. Thus, although default rates should certainly enter the negotiations regarding the premium to be paid, they should not be the sole factor in arriving at the final account.

In short, under the Old CSLP, the banks had a very good deal. They collected on the student loans that remained in good standing; they turned defaults over to the government and received full compensation for any losses incurred; and they gained access to an attractive postsecondary student client base. Now, under the New CSLP, the banks are assuming responsibility for the less-attractive student loans but retain the advantages of the better credit risks and of enhanced access to the desired client pool. By negotiating the flat 5 percent risk premium, an amount that presumably reflects the overall net value of student loan activities, the government has presumably been able to reach a fairer price for the overall package — to the benefit of the taxpayer. But no one can yet know if 5 percent is too much or too little. We suggest that close monitoring is in order, well before the five-year period of the agreement is over.

Borrowing Limits

Despite the recent increases in CSLP borrowing limits, we are still concerned about their adequacy. Some students need more than these amounts, and any failure to respond to this need will result in undue hardship and reduced access to postsecondary education. This consideration is especially important for students from lower-income families with limited access to other resources.

Furthermore, our empirical findings indicated that students generally seem to have been supply constrained in their borrowing. The suggestion is that they wanted to borrow more, and that repayment problems were not widespread, which means that they had the capacity to repay *even higher* levels of borrowing. Thus, the higher limits seem to appropriate and feasible.

On the other hand, our findings are based on historical analysis of borrowing and repayment under the lower limits and other conditions of the past decade. Thus, we recommend that any further increases in borrowing limits be monitored carefully to make sure students are not getting in over their heads.

Further Improvements

Although we generally judge the CSLP to be going in the right direction, the program is by no means perfect. Taking several more steps would provide some improvements and safeguards at fairly low cost.

A Pilot ICR System

Whatever one thinks of the New CSLP, the new arrangement with the banks will be in place until 2000, precluding any wholesale move to a federal ICR system in the near future. In this sense, ICR is simply off the federal policy agenda for the next few years. Under the new *Canada Student Financial Assistance Act*, however, the CSLP is allowed to conduct pilot projects for ICR loan programs with interested provinces.[2]

We suggest that a small-scale pilot system be initiated as soon as possible. It would have several rationales. One would be as a test. With an ICR system designed and put into place, analysts could assess its performance and compare the results with those of the New CSLP. The knowledge thus gained could then be used in making future policy decisions, including whether or not to move to a formal ICR system at the federal level or how the New CSLP might be further finetuned.

---

2 In its 1996 budget, Ontario announced that it was discussing a provincial ICR system with the federal government.

A second reason for instituting a pilot project is that the banks might perform just a little better knowing that their performance was going to be compared with that of the ICR alternative. Just as the growing interest in ICR probably contributed to the creation of the New CSLP, keeping the ICR option alive might lead to an enhanced performance of the current system.

A final reason is that a pilot ICR could provide extra funds for some students. We have already expressed concern about students who need financial assistance beyond what is available from the CSLP. A pilot ICR system could provide part of the solution.

Interest Relief and Loan Remission

We also recommend that the CSLP's provisions for interest relief for those who are unemployed or have low earnings be extended. As already noted, the program is not particularly costly, and a substantial expansion could be funded out of a small portion of the government's savings on default payments that accrue from the new arrangements with the banks.

That said, we emphasize that we generally like the basic design of the current program in that the student remains responsible for the outstanding principal and any accumulation of interest beyond the relief period. That is, the program should remain one that helps individuals get over certain early labor market humps and bumps; it should not be a program of long-term assistance.

In addition to providing direct benefits, the interest relief program should help with the assessment of the performance of the New CSLP. Two effects are possible but will need to be quantified. On the one hand, the hoped-for increases in repayment flexibility should result in fewer graduates' needing government assistance in repaying their loans. On the other hand, lending institutions may encourage potential defaulters to apply for interest relief as a means of forestalling losses. Thus, both the number of applications for relief and their underlying origin would provide useful information regarding the performance of the New CSLP and what it is likely to cost.

Although several provinces have programs that can forgive loans above certain limits, the CSLP has no loan remission program. The government might, however, consider a pilot program. Such an innovation would take the New CSLP one step closer toward being a near ICR-type system. Furthermore, just as it made sense to standardize need-assessment procedures across provinces, it would be reasonable to standardize the loan remission rules in a similar manner.

Need-Assessment Procedures

CSLP loans will continue to be issued to those deemed needy, but it is unclear how the recent streamlining of the eligibility criteria will affect who gets how much. Indeed, the past system is very difficult to evaluate in this regard. Despite the plenitude of anecdotal evidence suggesting that certain students have been able to exploit the system, there is no good empirical evidence on the extent of this problem. Our own analysis, for example, is limited to finding only that the loans system did not seem to be particularly progressive (that is, that there seemed to be no clear pattern in terms of students from lower-income families — measured by parental education — having received more assistance than those from better-off families).

We recognize this issue, which pertains to both the efficiency and the fairness of the system, as an important one. Given the lack of available information, our only recommendation is for a careful study of the issue, probably with the aid of new data better suited to such an evaluation. If such a study found that problems were indeed extensive, government could change the eligibility criteria and/or how they are applied.

More Data on Student Borrowing

The need for better data on student borrowing and repayment is obvious, especially given the major changes that have recently been instituted. We recommend that the government commit itself to a survey that would gather the sort of information already included in the NGS data bases *plus* much more detail about student borrowing.

In addition to information on the educational experience and early labor market outcomes, the data should include the following information on borrowers' backgrounds and their experience in taking out a loan:

- the individual's socioeconomic background;
- the individual's understanding of the CSLP;
- attitudes toward taking out loans for school and toward borrowing in general;
- anticipated earnings, debt load, and other aspects of the expected postschooling financial situation;
- the individual's experience with application procedures and the negotiation of the loan;
- the amount borrowed and the importance of the loan to the individual's postsecondary studies, including his or her access to alternative sources of financial assistance (such as family and jobs); and
- how the loan is spent.

The survey should also gather information on borrowers' experiences in repaying their loans, including:

- the individual's attitude toward borrowing from the perspective of the repayment period;
- the experience of negotiations over the repayment schedule;
- the bank's flexibility over the repayment period; and
- the burden of the loan repayments.

A longitudinal study based on a sample of students at various stages of their postsecondary careers would be best, but cross-sectional data with retrospective information would furnish some of this information at a significantly lower cost.

Postsecondary Education: The Big Picture

A recent report by the Association of Universities and Colleges of Canada (AUCC 1993) provides a summary of the current financial state of postsecondary education in Canada. One of its principal themes is that Canadian universities and colleges are currently in a fiscal crisis that is seriously compromising the quality of and access to higher education. This situation is seen to be the result of a period of steadily increasing enrollments (which recently ended) and declining government spending. The AUCC argues that universities and colleges have thus been forced to reduce the quality of education they offer and to limit access by restricting the number of students admitted to particular courses, programs, or institutions as a whole. This situation is not likely to improve in the foreseeable future.

Consider, however, that studies indicate that, as of the late 1980s (the date of the most recent comparative data available at time of writing), Canada was spending a higher percentage of its gross domestic product on postsecondary education and had a greater proportion of its population going on to the postsecondary level than any other nation of the Organisation for Economic Co-operation and Development (OECD 1992; 1993). At the same time, the OECD analysts judged the performance of the system less than commensurably superior; one of the reports concludes, "Canada spends a lot on education, but does not seem to be getting good value for money" (1992, 76).

The big questions need to be rethought. Who should go on to postsecondary studies, and what are the associated private and social benefits? What makes for a higher-quality education, and what quality are we willing to pay for? How should postsecondary education be funded, and how should it be priced? Should certain levels or fields of study be given preference over others? Is there a better way of delivering postsecondary education, such as eliminating duplicate programs, increasing (or decreasing) the integration of research and teaching, increasing (or decreasing) the number of "mini-career" programs, and so on? Could there be a re-ordering of the functions of the different types of postsecondary institutions — the universities, colleges, and trade and vocational schools? How does secondary schooling fit into these decisions? What of non-academic training programs?

In short, recent CSLP reforms have occurred largely in response to criticism of the Old CSLP and in the context of governments' budget-cutting agendas. Financial assistance for postsecondary students is, however, but one component of a much broader set of questions, and that whole range of issues needs to be addressed — with the student aid system comprising one component of that big picture.

Appendix A

Recent Changes in Provincial Aid Programs

The 1990s have been a period of rapid change in the Canadian system of financial assistance for postsecondary students. Since the federal government works together with provincial governments in this area, it is not surprising that, in addition to the changes to the Canada Student Loans Program (CSLP) discussed in the text, there have also been substantial changes to provincial student assistance programs. These programs vary significantly from one jurisdiction to another, and analyzing them in detail would be beyond the scope of this book. Instead, this appendix offers a summary of the most important recent changes at the provincial level as an introduction to these developments and as a way of putting our discussions of the CSLP in a broader context.

Changes from Grant to Loan Programs

As late as the 1990/91 academic year, almost all provinces gave needy students some form of grants or bursaries (the structure and generosity varied). By 1994/95, most of these aid packages had been eliminated, leaving behind only a scattering of grant programs aimed at fairly narrow subgroups of the student population. At the same time, borrowing from provincial student programs had increased significantly.

To illustrate the impact of these changes, Table A-1 shows the amounts of financial assistance issued in the forms of loans through the CSLP and provincial programs and the amounts of aid given in the form of grants by each jurisdiction participating in the CSLP (that is, all but Quebec and the Northwest Territories) in 1990/91 and in 1994/95.

In 1990/91, all but one province had grants programs in place, and they gave more than $250 million to postsecondary students; by 1995/96, programs still existed in only three provinces and Yukon Territory, and the amount of aid had fallen to just over $50 million. By contrast, in 1990/91, students borrowed more than $200 million from provincial loan programs; this amount had risen to just over $900 million by 1995/96 — almost 75 percent of what was borrowed from the CSLP in that year.

The changes in some individual provinces were even more dramatic. Before 1993/94, needy Ontario students were first given a provincial grant and then a federal loan; and a provincial loan was provided only if the other sources did not meet the assessed need. In 1993/94, the grant program was abolished, making CSLP loans the first type of aid offered, followed by a loan from the provincial program. Thus, grants fell from about $180 million to zero, while borrowing from the provincial program increased by a factor of ten to more than $550 million — 79 percent of the amount Ontario students borrowed from the CSLP.

The Maritime provinces had provided bursaries worth $47 million in 1990/91, but replaced them with loan programs. Consequently, borrowing in the four Atlantic provinces' programs increased from zero to $105 million between 1990/91 and 1994/95 — which was 75 percent of the level of CSLP borrowing). Manitoba eliminated its grants program and introduced a loan program that issued three times as much in loans as had been given away in the earlier period (57 percent the level of CSLP borrowing). In Alberta, one of the two general grant programs disappeared, while loans doubled (the new level representing 98 percent of CSLP borrowing).

The most important exception to this pattern was British Columbia, which maintained grant programs that give money to first- and second-year students; borrowing from the provincial program

Table A-1: *Federal and Provincial Student Financial Assistance,[a] fiscal years 1990/91 and 1994/95*

| | Canada Student Loans | | Provincial Aid | | | |
| | | | Loans | | Grants | |
	1990/91	1994/95	1990/91	1994/95	1990/91	1994/95
			(current $ millions)			
Newfoundland	36.36	51.70	0	32.87	16.23	0
Nova Scotia	43.55	50.37	0	45.00	14.05	0
Prince Edward Island	6.13	5.78	0	3.91	2.44	0
New Brunswick	39.24	32.71	0	23.85	14.86	4.17
Ontario	238.07	707.77	52.63	556.69	181.14	0
Manitoba	38.83	34.75	0	20.41	7.99	0
Saskatchewan	48.59	57.22	43.06	40.96	0	0
Alberta	114.10	114.65	61.81	112.22	39.52	22.25
British Columbia	100.13	174.35	51.29	65.68	27.88	24.61
Yukon	0.83	0.62	0	0	1.03	1.50
Total	*665.83*	*1,229.92*	*208.79*	*901.59*	*305.14*	*48.36*

[a] Omitting Quebec and the Northwest Territories.
[b] Data not available.

rose only moderately. The Yukon increased its small grant program (it had no loan program in either year). Saskatchewan was also an outlier: it had no grant program in either period and borrowing from the provincial program held approximately constant.

The switch from grants to loans did not necessarily result in savings for the provinces, since the loan programs are all subsidized, carry substantial interest costs for the governments, and have default costs in the form of either loan guarantees or risk-sharing premiums.

The principal burden of the cutbacks in grants has been borne largely by needy students who saw their bursaries replaced with loans. For them, the rising tuitions of the early 1990s were all the more burdensome since the provinces were reducing the available nonrepayable resources.

Procedures

Until 1994/95, each province had its own need-analysis rules, but by 1995/96, the standardized federal-provincial needs analysis laid out in the CSLP *Policy and Procedures Manual* (Canada 1995) had been adopted for the loan programs in all provinces except Ontario. The use of common procedures should assure that students will be treated equally in terms of qualifying for CSLP and provincial loan programs, regardless of where they live.

Provinces retain the right to designate which postsecondary institutions can be part of the CSLP. In most cases, institutions designated for CSLP eligibility are also designated for provincial loan program eligibility.

Risk Sharing with the
Financial Institutions

Several provinces have negotiated agreements with financial institutions similar to the one that characterizes the New CSLP discussed in the text. The banks receive a percentage of the value of each loan in return for accepting the responsibility for collection and the associated risk that borrowers might default. As in the federal program, the determination of loan eligibility remains under provincial jurisdiction so that aid is based on need rather than on ability to repay.

Loan Remission Programs

A number of provinces allow for loan forgiveness if the amounts borrowed exceed certain thresholds. The importance of these provisions has grown as high debt loads have become more common. The programs vary in whether they allow remission for all students with heavy annual debt burdens or only for those who have graduated from the institutions.

Appendix B

What Should Tuition Levels Be?

Policy discussions often link the student loan system and tuition levels. For example, one argument often made in favor of income contingent repayment (ICR) loan systems is that they could provide for increased borrowing on the part of students, allowing tuition to be raised to higher levels. Moreover, the increasing financial pressures on students resulting from recent tuition increases has made the search for ways of improving the student loan system all the more important.

In this study, we have attempted to keep the issues of tuition levels and the loan system separate, believing that one can discuss the qualities of a loan system in terms of how well it can deliver a *given* amount of assistance to those in need and that the question of tuition levels is beyond the scope of this volume. In this appendix, however, we summarize some of the major points likely to enter any debate about tuition levels and conclude by suggesting how they might be set. We do so in order to broaden the scope of the volume — even if only in an introductory manner — and to provide some ideas for future debates on the issue.

Who Pays for Postsecondary Education in Canada?

To set the stage, we return to the summary evidence presented in the text (Tables B-1, B-2, and B-3), which show that Canadian tuition levels and the proportion of instructional costs covered by tuition fees generally declined through the 1970s, rose moderately in the 1980s, increased more steeply in the early 1990s, and are generally scheduled to climb still further for at least the next few years. All told, tuition fees are now at levels substantially above those of the recent past and approximate the levels of the early 1960s.

From a broader perspective, it is important to understand that postsecondary education in Canada continues to be financed jointly by students (and their families) and the federal and provincial governments. *Despite* the recent increases in tuition, the larger share of the total costs are still paid out of the public purse. The greater part of tuition fees and living expenses, however, are borne by individuals and their families.

Thus, Canada continues to have a mixed public-private system of financing postsecondary education, and the policy debate largely revolves around the fine adjustments that should be made in the relative shares paid by society at large and by individuals and their families. No one seriously proposes moving wholesale in one direction or the other (a completely "free" system, as in certain European countries, or the "fully private" system of the private US universities).

The policy arguments for emphasizing one side or the other of the public-private mix are various, but most can be reduced to accenting one or both of the traditional economic criteria: efficiency and equity.

The Efficiency Aspects of Tuition Fees

The benefits of postsecondary education are both private and social. The private benefits, which accrue to individual students, include higher earnings than would otherwise be possible, the pleasure of learning, other monetary and nonmonetary benefits that flow from having a higher degree, and the educational experience itself.

The social benefits are difficult to fully define and generally impossible to estimate with any precision. They may include the political stability fostered by an informed electorate, the social cohesion that results from the transmission of a common culture, the

Table B-1: *Ratio of University Tuition Fees to Instructional Expenditures, academic years 1972/73 to 1993/94*

	Tuition Fees[a] (1)	Instructional Expenditures[b] (2)	Ratio (1)/(2)
		(current $ millions)	
1972/73	199	724	0.27
1973/74	209	787	0.27
1974/75	232	973	0.24
1975/76	253	1,168	0.22
1976/77	265	1,314	0.20
1977/78	290	1,458	0.20
1978/79	301	1,588	0.19
1979/80	324	1,712	0.20
1980/81	362	1,906	0.19
1981/82	423	2,126	0.20
1982/83	516	2,384	0.23
1983/84	576	2,536	0.23
1984/85	621	2,670	0.23
1985/86	661	2,836	0.23
1986/87	683	3,045	0.22
1987/88	747	3,241	0.23
1988/89	816	3,467	0.24
1989/90	902	3,760	0.24
1990/91	1,060	4,092	0.26
1991/92	1,264	4,425	0.29
1992/93	1,544	4,659	0.33
1993/94	1,570	4,601	0.34

[a] Includes fees for credit courses and miscellaneous fees, but excludes fees for noncredit courses.

[b] Total instructional and nonsponsored research expenditures, a standard category in these data that consists largely of academic salaries.

Source: Canadian Association of University Business Officers, *Financial Statistics of Universities and Colleges* (Ottawa: Statistics Canada for the Canadian Association of University Business Officers, various years).

Table B-2:   *Average University Tuition Fees,*
                   academic years 1970/71 to 1993/94

	Average Tuition
	(constant 1994 dollars)
1970/71	2,114
1971/72	2,155
1972/73	2,014
1973/74	1,817
1974/75	1,651
1975/76	1,564
1976/77	1,552
1977/78	1,436
1978/79	1,393
1979/80	1,371
1980/81	1,321
1981/82	1,355
1982/83	1,357
1983/84	1,387
1984/85	1,402
1985/86	1,399
1986/87	1,422
1987/88	1,430
1988/89	1,459
1989/90	1,622
1990/91	1,797
1991/92	1,921
1992/93	2,061
1993/94	2,250

Source: Association of Universities and Colleges of Canada, using data from Statistics Canada.

Table B-3: *Increases in University Tuition Fees, 1991–96*

	1991	1992	1993	1994	1995	1996
			(percent)			
Canada	16.9	8.5	9.2	9.4	7.3	11.8
Newfoundland	14.9	10.0	16.6	7.8	7.3	11.8
Prince Edward Island	13.8	8.4	9.1	5.6	7.5	5.3
Nova Scotia	13.2	9.9	10.3	9.4	7.7	8.9
New Brunswick	8.5	10.4	6.0	0.7	6.0	9.4
Quebec	43.8	10.6	6.0	9.1	0.3	0.6
Ontario	8.6	7.1	6.8	10.0	9.8	19.5
Manitoba	15.3	16.0	5.3	5.4	5.2	7.7
Saskatchewan	19.9	13.0	10.5	7.2	5.9	5.9
Alberta	15.0	17.5	21.4	12.9	10.7	9.7
British Columbia	10.9	1.0	10.1	8.3	5.7	1.6

Note: Increases are as at September of each year.

Source: Statistics Canada, *The Consumer Price Index*, cat. 62-001, September 1996.

reduced health costs accruing to a more informed public, a reduction in crime, and the external advantages of a more skilled and dynamic work force.[1]

Arguing for Efficiency

The discussion so far leads to an important element in the tuition debate: the issue of efficiency. At the margin, the personal and social

---

1 See Haveman and Wolfe (1984) for a full discussion of the public benefits of education.

benefits of a student engaged in postsecondary education should be worth the total costs of education; if not, the resources involved would be better directed elsewhere. Tuition fees have the key property of determining who goes on to postsecondary studies, and efficiency requires that the number who attend is just right — that is, exactly at the point at which the benefits are no longer greater than the costs.

By this reasoning, setting tuition too low wastes resources, as too many individuals (those for whom the benefits are not worth the costs) go on to postsecondary education, while setting it too high results in not enough attending, thus depriving society of a worthwhile investment in its human resources. The problem is, therefore, to find the tuition levels that cause individuals to make decisions based on their *own* best interests (the private benefits and costs) that bring the *total* of the private and social costs and benefits into line at the margin, resulting in the economically efficient amount of postsecondary education.[2]

Although this classic efficiency argument is quite straightforward in principle, putting it into practice is extremely challenging, especially when so many of the social benefits are so difficult to identify and measure in any precise manner. The opinion that the social benefits of postsecondary education are quite substantial has, however, long guided Canadian policy on the matter. Stager (1989, 98) reviews the findings of a number of provincial and federal commissions: "[t]he consensus that emerges...is that tuition fees should contribute about one-quarter to one-third of the total revenue for undergraduate education." But the alternative view has also been expressed, and West (1993), in reviewing the literature, finds the claims on behalf of significant social benefits to be amorphous, while

---

2 Most students, of course, would attend university regardless of any plausible changes in tuition. For them, the benefits of postsecondary education far exceed the benefits of working (and not going to school). Tuition rates that are "too high" or "too low" will only affect those students for whom working and postsecondary education are in close balance, so that small changes in costs and benefits can affect their decisions.

the 1974 Nova Scotia Commission justified their recommendation of full-cost tuition by asserting that most benefits were indeed private.

In summary, finding the right tuition level depends on correctly assessing the mix of private and social benefits. If the social benefits of postsecondary education are seen to far outweigh its private benefits, there is a strong argument for low tuition (or even paying students to go to school to compensate them for the earnings they must forgo). Conversely, if the social benefits are thought to be relatively small, one can argue that the burden of financing postsecondary education should fall primarily on students.

Assessing Efficiency

One established method of assessing the efficiency of tuition rates is to calculate the economic rate of return to postsecondary education and to compare this return with that of other investments, such as the returns to physical capital. For the past 30 years, economists have been studying these rates of return for various countries, for various subgroups within countries, and for various types of schooling. Summarizing this vast literature, Psacharopoulos (1994, 1328–1329) estimates the private rate of return at about 20 percent per year worldwide and at about 12 percent per year for the member countries of the Organisation for Economic Co-operation and Development (OECD). For Canada, Vaillancourt (1992) estimates it at about 8 percent per year.

These findings suugest that past tuition levels in Canada have not been too high, in the sense that the estimated 8 percent rate of return is generally above what individuals could have received from other forms of private investments such as stocks and bonds. Thus, postsecondary education has, on average, been a good investment for Canadians as individuals. Although raising tuition fees from the levels of the past decade or two might mean that fewer individuals go on to postsecondary studies, many would continue to do so.

Furthermore, to the degree the lower *private* rate of return in Canada versus other countries (8 percent versus 12 percent) indicates a lower *social* rate of return as well, this might suggest that tuition in

Canada has, in fact, been set too low from an efficiency perspective. That is, tuition rates have been low enough to generate a demand for education — and a corresponding supply of postsecondary graduates — sufficiently great to drive the rate of return to postsecondary education down to levels below those that prevail in other OECD countries.

Note, however, that such calculations are quite challenging to carry out, and the results typically depend to a great degree on the specific assumptions made regarding costs, future earnings, and so on. It is not at all clear that one can even begin to relate social rates of return to the private rates of return that have been estimated, and it is entirely the social rates of return that count when assessing the social efficiency of investments in postsecondary education. Such estimates represent broad brush strokes, and it is almost certain that some disciplines and levels of education have exceedingly high social rates of return while others have very low rates of return. Thus, the evidence on private rates of return is probably best taken as a rough starting point for discussion of the true private and, in particular, social rates of return to postsecondary education.

The Equity Arguments

An important caveat to the entire efficiency argument, however, is that it must be those with lesser *ability* — that is, those who stand to benefit less from postsecondary education — who are dissuaded from going on by higher levels of tuition. This consideration leads into the second major point regarding tuition levels: the equity arguments and the importance of ensuring access to the postsecondary system for those who have the ability and desire to attend.

Equal Access to Postsecondary Education

The first aspect of the equity issue is equality of opportunity: holding ability constant, the children of low-income parents should have the same educational opportunities as the children of higher-income parents. In Canada, this goal has been pursued by having post-secondary institutions admit all students deemed "academically able," regardless of family income, with governments then providing heavy subsidies to keep tuition fees relatively low and to provide loans and grants to those in need, thus keeping postsecondary education within the financial reach of all.

Keeping tuition fees low is, however, probably not a very effective means of trying to ensure equal access to the postsecondary system. First, low tuition rates across the board obviously keep costs down for *all* students, including those who could well afford to pay higher rates (a point we return to below). Second, the low tuition policy does not seem to have achieved its goal; even with these relatively low tuition policies in place, a disproportionately small number of postsecondary students have come from lower-income families (Porter and Jasmin 1987). Indeed, experience in countries that have abolished tuition completely indicates that students from upper-income families are still overrepresented (Woodhall 1989). In short, low tuition appears to be a blunt and ineffective tool for achieving equal access.

A better approach would probably be to institute programs that addressed the myriad attitudinal and related socioeconomic barriers, which are probably more responsible for limiting access for lower-income students, while, of course, also ensuring adequate financial assistance for those in need. As Levin notes:

> Financial barriers are not the primary obstacle to greater accessibility to universities....Accessibility could be improved more readily and more substantially through direct programmatic efforts than through indirect measures such as tuition policy. (1990, 51–52.)

Because the majority of provinces have eliminated their grants to needy students in the past few years (see Appendix A),[3] real tuition

---

3 British Columbia, Quebec, and Yukon Territory are the exceptions. Alberta's grant program continues but has been cut back.

fees for students from low-income families have been rising even faster than for others. We do not yet know how these increases have affected the proportion of low-income students who attend postsecondary education.

The Regressivity of Postsecondary Subsidies

Even if very low tuition effectively addressed the problem of access for low-income students, it might be judged inequitable for a different reason. Low tuition helps all students, regardless of their family income. But since postsecondary students come disproportionately from families in the upper reaches of the distribution of income, across-the-board assistance represents net subsidies from the average taxpayer to the children of those in the upper income range — a regressive transfer.[4] Furthermore, postsecondary graduates tend to have significantly higher lifetime earnings than others, making across-the-board subsidies of the system regressive over time as well.

Thus, the arguments made by student groups and others to keep tuition low in order to guarantee access to students from low-income families — although noble in appearance and perhaps equally laudable in intention — would turn out to be generally self-serving, while glossing over the regressive nature of the transfers being advocated.

Intergenerational Equity

Some people cite the fiscal realities of the times as a reason for raising tuition rates to levels higher than those of the past. Intergenerational equity considerations seem a mitigating factor here. How can one morally justify changing the rules of the postsecondary game? Are various high-tuition arguments that did not seem so compelling in the past suddenly so convincing?

---

4 Mehmet (1977; 1978), Meng and Sentance (1982), and Lemelin (1992) document the regressive nature of subsidies to postsecondary education.

Other Arguments

Any number of proposals concerning tuition levels have been put forward. We comment briefly on two.

Tuition Levels and
the Quality of Education

Arguments are sometimes advanced that higher tuition fees could result in a higher quality of education (or at least less of a decline) by providing additional funds to cash-strapped universities and colleges or by giving institutions financial incentives to provide higher quality instruction in order to attract more cash-bearing "clients" (see, for example, AUCC 1993).

These arguments are difficult to evaluate for several reasons. First, increased revenues from tuition increases might simply lead to offsetting declines in government transfers, thereby leaving unchanged the total money going to the postsecondary system. Second is the even more fundamental issue of the relationship between spending and quality. Would more money actually result in higher quality education? Finally, the "student-as-consumer" model presumes that students are the best judges of the quality of education — an assumption many educators question — and that financing schemes with the correct incentives could be devised. All these are things we do not know.

Tuition Fees That Vary by Program

The idea that fees should be set according to the private and social benefits and costs associated with a student's education can be applied not only to the overall tuition level but also across academic programs. Currently, the costs of educating students at different levels and in different programs vary widely, and social and private benefits also differ to a large degree. Yet tuition fees are relatively uniform. This situation appears to be inefficient (various fields and levels enroll the "wrong" number of students) as well as unfair (those who receive large private benefits from their education pay no more than others).

The opposition to greater differences in tuition fees by program or field of study is probably generally based on the notion that postsecondary education should simply be beyond such "crass" economic considerations on both the demand side and the supply side. That is, universities and colleges should not require one student to pay more than another simply because the costs or benefits of their programs differ. Neither should students face such price considerations when making their choices of higher learning. Such an approach would change the "feel" of the university — for the worse.

Furthermore, the practical problems would be great. If it is difficult to estimate the social and private benefits of postsecondary education in general, it is probably even tougher to do so at a more detailed level. Finally, substantial fee differentials would likely result in significant logistical problems, such as how to allocate money to faculties (or departments?) according to the principles underlying the pricing scheme.

Thus, although the idea of highly differential fees is alluring on grounds of both efficiency and fairness, there are counterarguments in terms of the nature of the university (or college) and the difficulty of putting into place and operating a system.

What Should Tuition Levels Be?

In the end, we share the widespread belief that postsecondary education provides substantial social benefits, difficult as these sometimes may be to identify and measure precisely. With regard to the equity arguments, it seems clear to us that low tuition is certainly not the only way to ensure access to the postsecondary system for children from low-income families, and we dislike the apparent regressivity of low tuition. The intergenerational argument is more compelling, as it is made on simple moral grounds. We consider the quality arguments too difficult to evaluate.

Thus, we think the standards proposed by earlier commissions (see Stager 1989) provide a good starting point. Their upper range would return the system to the historical norms of the late 1960s or early 1970s in terms of real tuition levels and the one-third of instruction costs (net of subsidies) that tuition fees would cover.

This conclusion leaves us approving of the rises of recent years, but advising caution with respect to further increases. At the same time, we believe that greater efforts need to be made to ensure equal access to the postsecondary system for those from low-income families, and that these initiatives should be directed at attitudes and other socioeconomic barriers as well as at providing adequate financial assistance. A limited move in the direction of differential fees for various fields, levels, and programs of study would be both feasible and justifiable on grounds of both efficiency and equity.

We also offer a relatively new idea for consideration: provide heavier subsidies (that is, lower tuition) for the first year or two of university, along with significantly greater funding for training and other nonacademic investment programs. Such a policy would provide strong incentives for individuals to begin to invest in their futures, while reducing the regressive nature of the current funding schemes by providing extra funding for the training options.

Appendix C

Regression Results

To analyze the effects of a variety of variables on the probability of a student's borrowing under a government loan program and of his or her making the required (or greater) payments during the two years after graduation, we estimated several multivariate regression models. All used data from Statistics Canada's National Graduates Surveys (NGS), covering students who graduated from Canadian colleges and universities in 1982, 1986, and 1990, interviewed two years later.

Given the following definitions, the samples revealed the characteristics reported in Table C-1, and our models yielded the results reported in Tables C-2 through C-5.

Dependent Variables

Having a student loan	Individual had an outstanding government (federal and/or provincial) student loan at graduation.
Amount borrowed	Amount owed to student loan program at graduation, in constant 1990 dollars. Defined only for those with loans (see above).
Proportion repaid	The proportion of the loan repaid as of the first interview. Constructed, by the authors, as one minus the amount owed divided by the amount owed at graduation (both amounts converted into constant 1990 dollars before making the calculation). Defined only for those with loans as of graduation.

| Difficulty with repayment | Individual reported difficulties with repayment of the student loan. Defined only for those who still had an outstanding student loan as of the interview. For the 1990 cohort, the variable refers to problems with government loan programs *per se*; for the 1986 cohort, the original question pertained to difficulties with either government or nongovernment student loans, but we restricted the universe to those with outstanding government loans as of the interview so as to have as a consistent measure for the two cohorts. |

Independent Variables

Field of study	Standard USIS categories, with some regrouping and disaggregation based on preliminary analysis of the data. Iin particular, we took Economics graduates from Social Sciences and put them with Commerce and Law graduates, and we separated Medicine graduates from Other Medical and Health graduates.
Age	Graduate's age as of the first interview (two years after graduation).
Province/region	In the borrowing models, the variables refer to the province or region of residence before enrollment in the education program (the province or region from which loan would have been granted). In the repayment models, the variables refer to residence at the time of interview. Preliminary analysis resulted in treating the Atlantic provinces as a single region and all other provinces separately.

Schooling characteristics

| Migration | Individual moved from one province to another to enroll in the education program. |

Part-time studies	Individual was enrolled part time at some point during the program.
Co-op	Individual graduated from a co-op program.
Re-entry	Individual had worked at least three years full time previous to enrolling in the program. (The three-year cutoff was chosen primarily to reduce the effects of the NGS having treated summer jobs slightly differently for the first two cohorts and the last.)
Normal length of program	Normal length of program, in years, on a full-time basis.

Parental education

Less than high school	Highest level of education was less than completed high school.
Less than completed BA	Highest education was more than high school but less than completed bachelor's degree or college diploma.
BA or higher	Highest level of education was bachelor's degree or higher.
Not stated	Parental education was not known or not given.

Marital and family status

Married	Individual was currently married (including common law).
Unmarried	Individual was separated, divorced, or widowed.
Presence of children	Children were present in the household.

Table C-1: *Sample Characteristics (Variable Means)*

	1982 Graduates		1986 Graduates		1990 Graduates	
	Male	Female	Male	Female	Male	Female
	(percent unless otherwise indicated; distributions may not add to 100 percent because of rounding)					
% with loans	46.5	42.6	44.3	41.1	48.0	44.4
Amount borrowed ($)[a]	5,010	5,410	7,130	6,750	8,800	8,760
% repaid	b	b	47.9	47.9	45.4	44.0
% with difficulty in repayment	b	b	25.6	26.9	19.2	25.6
Annual earnings ($)[a]	34,680	29,330	34,430	29,640	33,620	30,710
Age *(years)*	27.4	27.9	28.2	29.1	27.9	28.8
Province/region						
Atlantic Canada	9	11	6	7	8	10
Quebec	29	30	33	32	23	24
Ontario	36	34	40	39	42	40
Manitoba	4	4	3	4	4	5
Saskatchewan	4	5	4	4	5	5
Alberta	10	9	7	7	9	9
British Columbia	7	8	6	6	9	7
Schooling characteristics						
Moved to study	5	4	6	5	6	5
Part-time studies	20	27	23	32	22	26
Co-op	20	27	23	32	22	26
Re-entry	15	21	22	27	24	28
Normal length of program *(years)*	3.56	3.35	3.40	3.19	3.54	3.32

Table C-1 - continued

	1982 Graduates		1986 Graduates		1990 Graduates	
	Male	Female	Male	Female	Male	Female
	(percent unless otherwise indicated; distributions may not add to 100 percent because of rounding)					
Parental education						
Father: high school	47	49	34	37	31	36
Father: completed BA	29	28	35	34	35	33
Father: BA or higher	20	19	25	21	30	27
Father: not stated	4	4	6	8	4	4
Mother: high school	44	46	33	34	29	32
Mother: completed BA	43	42	49	51	49	50
Mother: BA or higher	9	9	12	10	18	15
Mother: not stated	4	3	6	5	4	3
Marital and family status						
Single	51	60	51	61	51	62
Married	45	39	45	37	44	36
Separated/ widowed/divorced	5	1	4	2	5	2
Presence of children	21	16	22	16	20	14

[a] Constant 1990 dollars.

[b] Data not available.

Table C-2: *Model I — Graduating with a Loan,*
Estimation Results

	1982 Graduates		1986 Graduates		1990 Graduates	
	Male	Female	Male	Female	Male	Female
Intercept	− 0.576**	0.881**	− 0.409**	1.454**	− 0.487**	0.229**
	(0.110)	(0.088)	(0.096)	(0.072)	(0.089)	(0.066)
Field of study						
Education	0.066	0.457**	0.194**	0.157**	0.310**	0.217**
	(0.041)	(0.030)	(0.039)	(0.027)	(0.034)	(0.025)
Fine arts & humanities	0.206**	0.168**	0.147**	0.023	0.006	0.249**
	(0.043)	(0.033)	(0.040)	(0.028)	(0.036)	(0.028)
Commerce, economics, law	0.027	0.148**	− 0.094**	− 0.055*	0.022	0.061**
	(0.034)	(0.035)	(0.035)	(0.029)	(0.029)	(0.027)
Agriculture & biosciences	0.173**	0.240**	0.105*	0.347**	0.094**	0.300**
	(0.054)	(0.048)	(0.054)	(0.044)	(0.047)	(0.037)
Engineering	0.124**	0.075	0.186**	0.334**	0.164**	0.208**
	(0.037)	(0.068)	(0.037)	(0.063)	(0.033)	(0.058)
Doctors	0.898**	0.241**	0.713**	0.607**	0.300**	0.599**
	(0.065)	(0.056)	(0.058)	(0.055)	(0.052)	(0.046)
Other medical & health	− 0.041	0.292**	0.025	0.036	− 0.023	− 0.004
	(0.188)	(0.039)	(0.100)	(0.033)	(0.100)	(0.032)
Maths & physical sciences	− 0.080*	− 0.056	− 0.020	− 0.064	− 0.092**	0.027
	(0.043)	(0.056)	(0.039)	(0.046)	(0.037)	(0.048)
Age	0.006	− 0.061**	0.005*	− 0.053**	− 0.005*	− 0.027**
	(0.004)	(0.003)	(0.003)	(0.002)	(0.003)	(0.002)
Province/region						
Atlantic Canada	0.617**	0.626**	0.615**	0.331**	0.769**	0.772**
	(0.037)	(0.034)	(0.040)	(0.034)	(0.035)	(0.029)
Quebec	− 0.011	0.250**	0.279**	− 0.065**	0.408**	0.589**
	(0.025)	(0.025)	(0.024)	(0.022)	(0.023)	(0.021)
Manitoba	− 0.268**	− 0.054	− 0.242**	− 0.333**	0.139**	0.280**
	(0.054)	(0.050)	(0.053)	(0.047)	(0.043)	(0.039)
Saskatchewan	0.015	− 0.135**	− 0.211**	− 0.281**	0.245**	0.299**
	(0.050)	(0.048)	(0.050)	(0.045)	(0.041)	(0.037)
Alberta	0.186**	0.288**	0.471**	0.239**	0.613**	0.650**
	(0.036)	(0.036)	(0.039)	(0.035)	(0.032)	(0.030)
British Columbia	0.044	0.340**	− 0.016	− 0.171**	0.175**	0.148**
	(0.041)	(0.039)	(0.040)	(0.037)	(0.033)	(0.033)

Table C-2 - continued

	1982 Graduates		1986 Graduates		1990 Graduates	
	Male	Female	Male	Female	Male	Female
Schooling characteristics						
Moved to study	0.301**	0.081*	0.087**	0.548**	0.091**	0.198**
	(0.044)	(0.049)	(0.041)	(0.038)	(0.038)	(0.036)
Part-time studies	− 0.191**	− 0.208**	− 0.504**	− 0.378**	− 0.274**	− 0.531**
	(0.028)	(0.026)	(0.025)	(0.023)	(0.023)	(0.022)
Co-op	− 0.042	0.027	− 0.104**	− 0.338**	− 0.095**	0.085**
	(0.036)	(0.034)	(0.041)	(0.061)	(0.032)	(0.042)
Re-entry	− 0.280**	0.093**	− 0.415**	− 0.092**	− 0.104**	0.015
	(0.041)	(0.037)	(0.035)	(0.030)	(0.026)	(0.024)
Normal length of program (+1 year)	0.076**	0.100**	0.084**	0.039**	0.101**	0.061**
	(0.013)	(0.011)	(0.011)	(0.009)	(0.012)	(0.010)
Parental education						
Father: high school completed	0.066**	− 0.060**	− 0.141**	− 0.196**	0.083**	− 0.177**
	(0.028)	(0.026)	(0.025)	(0.023)	(0.025)	(0.022)
Father: BA or higher	− 0.251**	− 0.331**	− 0.452**	− 0.389**	− 0.152**	− 0.309**
	(0.033)	(0.031)	(0.030)	(0.027)	(0.028)	(0.025)
Father: not stated	− 0.619**	0.403**	0.174**	0.010	0.074	0.216**
	(0.082)	(0.065)	(0.050)	(0.041)	(0.063)	(0.054)
Mother: high school completed	− 0.010	− 0.119**	− 0.075**	− 0.127**	0.064**	0.013
	(0.027)	(0.025)	(0.025)	(0.022)	(0.024)	(0.021)
Mother: BA or higher	0.093**	0.113**	0.035	− 0.272**	− 0.182**	− 0.088**
	(0.043)	(0.041)	(0.037)	(0.034)	(0.033)	(0.030)
Mother: not stated	0.321**	− 0.472**	− 0.332**	− 0.157**	− 0.213**	− 0.587**
	(0.083)	(0.073)	(0.052)	(0.049)	(0.064)	(0.063)
Number of observations	2,210	2,380	2,420	2,890	2,380	2,850
Log likelihood	− 11,366	− 12,142	− 13,146	− 15,394	− 14,511	− 17,187

Note: Probit model (0-1) of graduating with a loan.

* Significantly different from zero at the 0.10 confidence level.

** Significantly different from zero at the 0.05 confidence level.

Table C-3: Model II — Amount Borrowed, Estimation Results

	1982 Graduates		1986 Graduates		1990 Graduates	
	Male	Female	Male	Female	Male	Female
Intercept	− 3,897**	1,001	4,398*	366.4	− 1,141	982.3
	(1,710)	(1,300)	(2,284)	(1,269)	(1,810)	(1,346)
Field of study						
Education	1,986**	589.2	540.4	1,078**	1,735**	1,197**
	(517.2)	(367.2)	(865.3)	(389.9)	(616.5)	(467.4)
Fine arts & humanities	433.7	263.0	394.8	693.6	768.8	− 872.8*
	(527.3)	(435.0)	(900.6)	(425.9)	(697.3)	(525.8)
Commerce, economics, law	847.2*	− 209.2	1,715.3**	655.7	1,612**	1,329**
	(432.3)	(445.8)	(791.0)	(433.1)	(554.2)	(507.3)
Agriculture & biosciences	1,440**	1,001*	− 768.4	1,155**	1,282	1,534**
	(646.8)	(578.1)	(1,187)	(579.2)	(870.4)	(664.8)
Engineering	1,204**	− 157.1	− 408.4	− 611.8	592.5	1,209
	(459.7)	(854.9)	(810.3)	(835.2)	(608.2)	(976.3)
Doctors	4,671**	916.6	3,085**	2,284**	4,712**	4,221**
	(616.4)	(662.9)	(1,053)	(660.8)	(873.5)	(723.7)
Other medical & health	− 582.9	436.8	− 358.5	398.0	1,812	1,329**
	(2,472)	(472.2)	(2,375)	(490.3)	(1,885)	(611.1)
Maths & physical sciences	804.4	103.4	− 1,240	373.8	422.8	1,456
	(548.8)	(737.5)	(898.3)	(709.6)	(710.5)	(885.5)
Age	291.0**	114.4**	163.8**	254.6**	320.3**	173.0**
	(57.9)	(45.3)	(71.8)	(42.3)	(54.6)	(41.0)
Province/region						
Atlantic Canada	464.4	1,658**	− 25.01	1,172**	2,270**	2,856**
	(384.3)	(364.6)	(753.3)	(435.7)	(548.9)	(479.0)
Quebec	375.8	1,005**	− 2,228**	− 1,868**	− 610.0	890.1**
	(313.2)	(311.9)	(507.6)	(331.2)	(432.9)	(384.5)
Manitoba	− 834.3	1,121**	− 1,696	− 1,464**	306.3	1,308*
	(739.3)	(658.2)	(1,316)	(735.2)	(842.4)	(732.4)
Saskatchewan	− 797.7	− 279.9	− 3,284**	− 1,414**	2,619**	3,688**
	(609.1)	(620.2)	(1,212)	(715.9)	(755.6)	(697.5)
Alberta	386.5	906.4*	− 492.2	− 115.5	1,131**	1,689**
	(417.0)	(427.8)	(761.0)	(461.8)	(539.2)	(506.7)
British Columbia	− 683.8	612.6	− 1,239	330.4	1,333**	1,753**
	(484.0)	(454.9)	(910.9)	(563.3)	(634.4)	(632.3)

Table C-3 - continued

	1982 Graduates		1986 Graduates		1990 Graduates	
	Male	Female	Male	Female	Male	Female
Schooling characteristics						
Moved to study	589.9	192.6	− 1,094	555.0	1,647**	1,345**
	(460.0)	(535.6)	(886.0)	(477.8)	(655.5)	(590.1)
Part-time studies	− 132.3	− 939.2**	− 72.59	− 669.5*	− 985.7**	− 849.9**
	(312.3)	(348.1)	(591.5)	(344.5)	(435.6)	(410.0)
Co-op	− 86.68	− 284.67	− 2,038**	− 1,661*	− 1,141**	− 1,298*
	(425.2)	(388.2)	(868.9)	(963.7)	(581.0)	(725.5)
Re-entry	− 631.4	− 615.4	− 2,405**	− 875.6*	− 720.4	− 71.0
	(483.4)	(444.9)	(763.3)	(451.9)	(471.7)	(424.1)
Normal length of program (+1 year)	144.7	107.0	− 191.8	− 6.9	120.4	380.3**
	(158.0)	(134.9)	(240.8)	(132.3)	(219.1)	(179.5)
Parental education						
Father: high school completed	307.5	325.8	− 232.5	− 202.8	− 959.0**	− 103.5
	(327.1)	(317.2)	(541.2)	(320.8)	(432.3)	(374.6)
Father: BA or higher	− 488.4	− 35.59	708.1	− 1,303**	− 765.7	− 935.7**
	(427.7)	(395.4)	(670.7)	(404.0)	(511.7)	(445.4)
Father: not stated	2,171**	846.3	− 149.4	58.66	− 24.01	2,835**
	(997.7)	(674.4)	(981.8)	(599.8)	(1,109)	(863.3)
Mother: high school completed	− 584.6*	− 497.9*	− 702.1	− 309.5	− 208.2	− 231.1
	(320.4)	(297.0)	(530.1)	(313.9)	(420.6)	(364.1)
Mother: BA or higher	− 551.2	− 904.6*	1,271	265.8	− 533.7	− 291.7
	(536.8)	(478.0)	(796.2)	(516.1)	(613.5)	(547.2)
Mother: not stated	− 2,752**	− 1,205	3,292**	− 155.9	597.4	− 2,259**
	(913.0)	(827.2)	(1,108)	(751.4)	(1,135)	(1,119)
Number of observations	1,100	1,090	1,190	1,320	1,270	1,420
R^2	0.118	0.054	0.088	0.106	0.128	0.123

Note: Ordinary least squares model of amount of loan, estimated for those with loans.

* Significantly different from zero at the 0.10 confidence level.

** Significantly different from zero at the 0.05 confidence level.

Table C-4: *Model III — Proportion Repaid,*
Estimation Results

	1986 Graduates		1990 Graduates	
	Male	Female	Male	Female
Intercept	0.434**	0.811**	0.792**	0.805**
	(0.064)	(0.051)	(0.059)	(0.047)
Field of study				
Education	− 0.007	− 0.061**	− 0.012	0.034**
	(0.024)	(0.015)	(0.019)	(0.015)
Fine arts & humanities	− 0.090**	− 0.105**	0.035	0.070**
	(0.025)	(0.016)	(0.022)	(0.017)
Commerce, economics, law	− 0.020	− 0.069**	− 0.020	0.086**
	(0.022)	(0.016)	(0.017)	(0.016)
Agriculture & biosciences	0.107**	− 0.004	0.092**	0.139**
	(0.033)	(0.022)	(0.028)	(0.022)
Engineering	0.188**	− 0.010	0.084**	0.316**
	(0.023)	(0.033)	(0.019)	(0.032)
Doctors	0.057*	0.096**	0.151**	0.179**
	(0.032)	(0.027)	(0.028)	(0.025)
Other medical & health	0.261**	0.073**	− 0.030	0.205**
	(0.066)	(0.019)	(0.059)	(0.020)
Maths & physical sciences	0.030	0.0004	0.036*	0.174**
	(0.025)	(0.027)	(0.022)	(0.029)
Age	0.003	− 0.0003	− 0.004**	− 0.002
	(0.002)	(0.002)	(0.002)	(0.001)
Amount borrowed (+$1,000)	− 0.010**	− 0.032**	− 0.029**	− 0.028**
	(0.001)	(0.001)	(0.001)	(0.001)
Annual earnings (+$1,000)	0.003**	0.002**	0.003**	0.003**
	(0.000)	(0.000)	(0.000)	(0.000)
Province/region				
Atlantic Canada	− 0.144**	− 0.191**	− 0.067**	− 0.127**
	(0.021)	(0.016)	(0.018)	(0.017)
Quebec	− 0.148**	− 0.156**	− 0.063**	− 0.219**
	(0.014)	(0.012)	(0.013)	(0.012)
Manitoba	− 0.040	− 0.051**	0.002	0.006
	(0.034)	(0.025)	(0.028)	(0.026)
Saskatchewan	− 0.054*	− 0.069**	− 0.027	0.030
	(0.032)	(0.028)	(0.026)	(0.025)
Alberta	− 0.026	− 0.020	0.051**	0.011
	(0.020)	(0.017)	(0.016)	(0.015)
British Columbia	− 0.043*	0.031	0.062**	− 0.050**
	(0.023)	(0.019)	(0.019)	(0.018)

Table C-4 - continued

	1986 Graduates		1990 Graduates	
	Male	Female	Male	Female
Schooling characteristics				
Moved to study	− 0.170**	− 0.075**	− 0.054**	− 0.019
	(0.023)	(0.017)	(0.021)	(0.018)
Part-time studies	0.131**	0.150**	0.071**	0.129**
	(0.016)	(0.013)	(0.013)	(0.013)
Co-op	0.063**	− 0.208**	0.074**	− 0.009
	(0.024)	(0.037)	(0.018)	(0.023)
Re-entry	0.051**	− 0.089**	0.068**	0.013
	(0.022)	(0.018)	(0.015)	(0.014)
Normal length of program (+1 year)	0.012*	0.008	− 0.018**	− 0.013**
	(0.007)	(0.005)	(0.007)	(0.006)
Parental education				
F ather: high school completed	0.009	− 0.047**	− 0.024	− 0.049**
	(0.015)	(0.012)	(0.013)	(0.012)
Father: BA or higher	0.005	0.012	− 0.035**	− 0.114**
	(0.019)	(0.015)	(0.016)	(0.014)
Father: not stated	− 0.024	− 0.035	− 0.140**	− 0.056**
	(0.027)	(0.023)	(0.034)	(0.028)
Mother: high school completed	− 0.005	0.041**	0.038**	− 0.030**
	(0.015)	(0.012)	(0.013)	(0.012)
Mother: BA or higher	− 0.081**	0.020	0.036*	− 0.056**
	(0.022)	(0.020)	(0.019)	(0.017)
Mother: not stated	− 0.005	0.041	0.179**	0.054
	(0.031)	(0.029)	(0.035)	(0.039)
Marital and family status				
Married	0.080**	0.065**	− 0.048**	− 0.044**
	(0.013)	(0.011)	(0.011)	(0.010)
Separated/widowed/divorced	− 0.063	− 0.134**	0.171**	0.062**
	(0.043)	(0.026)	(0.039)	(0.026)
Presence of children	− 0.131**	− 0.016	− 0.014	− 0.061**
	(0.020)	(0.016)	(0.017)	(0.016)
Number of observations	1,120	1,260	1,100	1,180
Log likelihood	− 7,237	− 7,649	− 7,035	− 7,888

Note: Two-sided tobit model of the proportion of the loan repaid at the time of the first interview, two years after graduation.

* Significantly different from zero at the 0.10 confidence level.

** Significantly different from zero at the 0.05 confidence level.

Table C-5: *Model IV — Difficulties with Repayment, Estimation Results*

	1986 Graduates		1990 Graduates	
	Male	Female	Male	Female
Intercept	− 1.582**	− 1.333**	− 2.659**	− 1.667**
	(0.219)	(0.188)	(0.214)	(0.164)
Field of study				
Education	− 0.415**	− 0.267**	− 0.197**	− 0.076
	(0.077)	(0.055)	(0.070)	(0.052)
Fine arts & humanities	0.369**	− 0.129**	0.443**	0.249**
	(0.074)	(0.060)	(0.077)	(0.058)
Commerce, economics, law	− 0.506**	− 0.228**	− 0.018	− 0.005
	(0.069)	(0.061)	(0.063)	(0.057)
Agriculture & biosciences	− 1.193**	− 0.426**	0.190*	0.104
	(0.136)	(0.088)	(0.103)	(0.075)
Engineering	− 0.706**	− 0.436**	0.114	0.302**
	(0.078)	(0.140)	(0.072)	(0.121)
Doctors	− 0.649**	− 0.600**	− 0.539**	− 0.634**
	(0.117)	(0.131)	(0.119)	(0.116)
Other medical & health	*a*	− 0.571**	*a*	− 0.565**
	a	(0.081)	*a*	(0.088)
Maths & physical sciences	− 0.394**	− 0.788**	0.022	− 0.070
	(0.083)	(0.114)	(0.084)	(0.110)
Age	0.047**	0.043**	0.042**	0.054**
	(0.007)	(0.006)	(0.007)	(0.005)
Amount borrowed (+$1,000)	0.013**	0.058**	0.039**	0.043*
	(0.002)	(0.003)	(0.003)	(0.003)
Annual earnings (+$1,000)	− 0.010**	− 0.030**	− 0.003**	− 0.030**
	(0.001)	(0.002)	(0.001)	(0.001)
Province/region				
Atlantic Canada	− 0.283**	− 0.093	0.086	− 0.390**
	(0.071)	(0.060)	(0.065)	(0.059)
Quebec	− 0.252**	− 0.176**	− 0.353**	− 0.698**
	(0.050)	(0.048)	(0.058)	(0.048)
Manitoba	− 0.439**	0.497**	0.560**	− 0.538**
	(0.117)	(0.090)	(0.094)	(0.097)
Saskatchewan	− 0.149	− 0.808**	0.215**	− 0.017
	(0.103)	(0.152)	(0.090)	(0.084)
Alberta	− 0.375**	− 0.177**	0.275**	− 0.546**
	(0.070)	(0.065)	(0.056)	(0.057)
British Columbia	− 0.285**	0.413**	0.472**	− 0.004
	(0.077)	(0.070)	(0.066)	(0.061)

Table C-5 - continued

	1986 Graduates		1990 Graduates	
	Male	Female	Male	Female
Schooling characteristics				
Moved to study	0.248**	0.052	0.133*	0.232**
	(0.072)	(0.062)	(0.070)	(0.061)
Part-time studies	0.149**	0.125**	0.303**	− 0.122**
	(0.055)	(0.050)	(0.047)	(0.048)
Co-op	− 0.110	0.449**	− 0.262**	− 0.589**
	(0.098)	(0.150)	(0.080)	(0.106)
Re-entry	0.186**	0.022	− 0.164**	0.119**
	(0.071)	(0.060)	(0.056)	(0.049)
Normal length of program (+1 year)	0.162**	− 0.072**	0.078**	0.040**
	(0.024)	(0.019)	(0.027)	(0.020)
Parental education				
Father: high school completed	− 0.218**	− 0.220**	− 0.096*	− 0.006
	(0.054)	(0.046)	(0.049)	(0.044)
Father: BA or higher	0.169**	0.017	− 0.135**	0.159**
	(0.063)	(0.058)	(0.058)	(0.052)
Father: not stated	0.178**	− 0.290**	0.033	0.145**
	(0.089)	(0.087)	(0.130)	(0.099)
Mother: high school completed	− 0.053	0.149**	0.085*	− 0.066
	(0.053)	(0.045)	(0.048)	(0.043)
Mother: BA or higher	− 0.229**	0.549**	− 0.006	− 0.061
	(0.075)	(0.069)	(0.074)	(0.063)
Mother: not stated	− 0.502**	0.451**	− 0.275*	− 0.670**
	(0.121)	(0.110)	(0.165)	(0.166)
Marital and family status				
Married	− 0.682**	− 0.370**	− 0.384**	− 0.180**
	(0.052)	(0.042)	(0.046)	(0.038)
Separated/widowed/divorced	0.560**	0.561**	0.766**	− 0.119
	(0.127)	(0.092)	(0.140)	(0.088)
Presence of children	0.449**	0.554**	0.353**	0.095*
	(0.071)	(0.056)	(0.062)	(0.056)
Number of observations	820	930	850	940
Log likelihood	− 2,967	− 3,465	− 3,052	− 3,811

Note: Probit model (0-1) of self-reported difficulties with repayment, estimated for those with outstanding loans as of the first interview, two years after graduation.

[a] Too few observations to be reported.

* Significantly different from zero at the 0.10 confidence level.

** Significantly different from zero at the 0.05 confidence level.

References

Association of Universities and Colleges of Canada (AUCC). 1993. "A New Student Assistance Plan for Canada." A report by the AUCC Standing Advisory Committee on Funding. Ottawa.

Bennecon Ltd. 1991. "Assessing Need in the Canadian Student Loans Program." [Toronto?]. Mimeographed.

Bovey Commission. *See* Commission on the Future Development of the Universities of Ontario.

Canada. 1985. Royal Commission on the Economic Union and Development Prospects for Canada. *Report*, 3 v. Chair was Donald Macdonald. Ottawa: Supply and Services Canada.

———. 1990. Auditor-General. *Report of the Auditor-General of Canada to the House of Commons*. Ottawa.

———. 1993. Department of the Secretary of State. *Request for Financing Canada Student Loans*. Ottawa.

———. 1994a. Canada Student Loan Program. *Policy and Procedures Manual*. Ottawa.

———. 1994b. Department of Human Resources Development. *Improving Social Security: A Discussion Paper*. Ottawa.

———. 1995. *1995-96 Estimates, Part III, Expenditure Plan*. Ottawa: Supply and Services Canada.

———. 1996a. *1996-97 Estimates, Part III, Expenditure Plan*. Ottawa: Supply and Services Canada.

———. 1996b. Department of Human Resources Development. *Evaluation and Data Development, Request for Proposals: Evaluation Framework, Canada Student Loans Program*, Annex A. Ottawa.

Commission on the Future Development of the Universities of Ontario. 1984. *Ontario Universities: Options and Futures*. Chair was Gerald Bovey. Toronto.

Duncan, Caryn. 1992. *Compromising Access*. Ottawa: Canadian Federation of Students.

———. 1993. "Squeezing Out Students." In Edwin G. West, *Ending the Squeeze on Universities*. Montreal: Institute for Research on Public Policy.

Finnie, Ross. 1994. "Student Loans in Canada: A Cross-Cohort Micro Analysis of Borrowing and Repayment Patterns of University and College Graduates." Research report prepared for Industry Canada, Science Promotion and Academic Affairs Branch. Ottawa. With the assistance of Gaétan Garneau.

———, and Gaétan Garneau. 1996a. "An Analysis of Student Borrowing for Post-Secondary Education." *Canadian Business Economics* 4 (2): 51–64.

———, and Gaétan Garneau. 1996b. "Student Borrowing for Post-Secondary Education." *Educational Quarterly Review* 3 (2): 7–34.

———, and Saul Schwartz. 1996. "Student Loans in Canada: An Econometric Analysis." Carleton University, School of Public Administration. Ottawa.

Friedman, Milton. 1962. "The Role of Government in Higher Education." In Milton Friedman, *Capitalism and Freedom*. Chicago: University of Chicago Press.

Haveman, Robert, H., and Barbara L. Wolfe. 1984. "Schooling and Economic Well-Being: The Role of Nonmarket Effects." *Journal of Human Resources* 19 (summer): 377–407.

Kesselman, Jonathan R. 1993. "Squeezing Universities, Students, or Taxpayers?" In Edwin G. West, *Ending the Squeeze on Universities*. Montreal: Institute for Research on Public Policy.

Kruger, Alan B., and William G. Bowen. 1993. "Income-Contingent College Loans." *Journal of Economic Perspectives* 7 (3): 193–202.

Lemelin, Clément. 1992. "Short-Term Redistributive Effects of Public Financing of University Education in Quebec." *Canadian Public Policy* 18 (2): 176–188.

Levin, Benjamin. 1990. "Tuition Fees and University Accessibility." *Canadian Public Policy* 16 (1): 51–59.

Macdonald Commission. *See* Canada 1985.

Mankiw, N. Gregory. 1986. "The Allocation of Credit and Financial Collapse." *Quarterly Journal of Economics* 100 (August): 455–470.

Mehmet, Ozay. 1977. "Economic Returns to Undergraduate Fields of Study in Canadian Universities: 1961 to 1972." *Industrial Relations* 32 (3): 321–339.

————. 1978. *Who Benefits From the Ontario University System?* Occasional Paper 7. Toronto: Ontario Economic Council.

Meng, Ronald, and Jim Sentance. 1982. "Canadian Universities: Who Benefits and Who Pays?" *Canadian Journal of Higher Education* 12 (3): 47–58.

Nova Scotia. 1974. Royal Commission of Education, Public Services and Provincial-Municipal Relations. *Report*. Halifax.

Organisation for Economic Co-operation and Development (OECD). 1992. *Economic Surveys: Canada*. Paris: OECD.

————. 1993. *Education at a Glance*. Paris: OECD, Centre for Educational Research and Innovation.

Porter, Marion, and Gilles Jasmin. 1987. "A Profile of Post-Secondary Students in Canada." Ottawa: Secretary of State.

Psacharopoulos, George. 1994. "Returns to Investment in Education — A Global Update." *World Development* 22 (9): 1325–1343.

Stager, David. 1989. *Focus on Fees: Alternative Policies for University Tuition Fees*. Toronto: Council of Ontario Universities.

————, and Dan Derkach. 1992. *Contingent Repayment Student Assistance Plans*. Toronto: Council of Ontario Universities.

Students' Union of Nova Scotia. 1994. "Downloading Canada's Debt: The Social and Economic Implications of an Income Contingent Loan Repayment Programme in Canada." Halifax.

Vaillancourt, François. 1995. "The Private and Total Returns to Education in Canada, 1985." *Canadian Journal of Economics* 28 (3): 532–554.

West, Edwin. 1993. *Ending the Squeeze on Universities*. Montreal: Institute for Research on Public Policy.

Woodhall, Maureen. 1989. "Loans for Learning: The Loans versus Grants Debate in International Perspective." *Higher Educational Quarterly* 43 (1): 76–87.

An Income Contingent Repayment Scheme:

A Plea for Canada's Students

Bruce Chapman

Perhaps the most significant current debate in higher education internationally concerns student finances. The essential question is, what is the best way to organize, deliver, and fund assistance to higher education students? The analysis of Ross Finnie and Saul Schwartz addresses the issue in the Canadian context.

The policy question has become pertinent for a host of factors that are being felt both in Canada and elsewhere. They include the expansion in demand for university services; fiscal parsimony, suggesting that governments today are unwilling to fund public services by increases in general taxation; and, concomitantly, an increasing reluctance to accept old methods if they are seen to be inefficient or too reliant on the public purse.

Finnie and Schwartz provide a thoughtful and informative examination of the nature, significance, and relative strengths and weaknesses of the Canada Student Loans Program (CSLP), in both its old and new formats. The study not only addresses the pluses and minuses of the schemes but also offers empirical analysis of the characteristics of borrowers and assessment of the potential benefits of a very different approach — income contingent repayment (ICR) schemes. It should be compulsory reading for anyone interested in the Canadian student finances debate or, indeed, higher education loans and charges generally.

In what follows, I focus my commentary on what might have been improved in the study and on what has been omitted, rather than on the much larger number of positive contributions that will be obvious to most readers. A reviewer's task is essentially that of constructive critic.

I should declare my views early in this review. I am a strong supporter of ICR, believing that a proper understanding of the economics of education leads inexorably to its promotion. The Australian experience with an ICR mechanism — the Higher Education Contribution Scheme (HECS) — demonstrates that it is administratively feasible and both economically and socially desirable. The CSLP will always need improvement so long as its fundamental arrangements are based on a model different from ICR.

The Australian System

Before proceeding, it is useful to outline the nature of the Australian higher education financing system, given that much of my review derives explicitly and implicitly from comparisons between a working ICR system and what have been and will be the Canadian approaches.

The Australian arrangements have two dimensions relevant to this comment: the charge system, HECS; and student income support policy, AUSTUDY.[1]

HECS is a compulsory uniform charge levied on all Australian undergraduates. It equals about 25 percent of average course costs, or approximately $2,500 per full-time year.[2] Students have the option of paying the charge upon enrollment, which attracts a 25 percent discount (that is, the charge for up-front payees is about $1,900).

---

1 The information in this section relates to the current (1996) Australian arrangements. In August 1996, the new government announced significant changes to the HECS system to be introduced in 1997. They include charges differentials depending on the course studied, and a lowering of the first income threshold at which repayment of the debt begins.

2 The Canadian and Australian dollars have rough parity, so for simplicity's sake I simply report actual money amounts without specifying Australian dollars or converting to Canadian currency.

About a quarter of undergraduates take this financial route, currently delivering to the government about $150 million per year (roughly 3 percent of total higher education revenue).

An important reason the majority of students choose to pay later is that the HECS debt has a zero real rate of interest. Thus, for many, even a discount of 25 percent does not make the up-front option attractive.

Payment for students who choose to defer operates through the tax system. The debt is collected only when and if a former student earns the average income of Australians working for pay — about $28,000 per year. The repayments are at rates in proportion to income, starting at 3 percent (that is, the HECS debt is reduced by about $850 per year at the first level of income). On average, a typical student takes about ten years to repay his or her HECS debt.

Student income support takes the form of grants that are means tested on the basis of family income. About half the student body qualify for some AUSTUDY.

An interesting innovation, which could be relevant to future Canadian reforms, is the AUSTUDY Loans Supplement, which allows a student in receipt of support to trade in his or her grant for an ICR loan at a ratio of 1:2.[3] If the student takes this option, the debt is repaid in the same way and at about the same rates as HECS. The supplement was designed to increase the flexibility of delivery of student finances without increasing government outlays.[4]

Tuition and the Benefits of Higher Education

Ironically, one of the best themes in the Finnie and Schwartz study appears explicitly only in an appendix (although it informs much of the rest of the work). It is the fact that the authors endorse the economics of education as the appropriate way to think about Cana-

3 About 15 percent of students in receipt of AUSTUDY currently take up the option.

4 For discussion and analysis of the supplement, see Chapman (1992).

dian student loans. From this reviewer's perspective, this paradigm is the correct one, and, with some exceptions, it is done well.

Much of Appendix B is a discussion of the relevance of private versus external benefits and what this implies for the overall level of public subsidy. An important point here is what role assessments of the social costs and benefits should play in deciding tuition charges, which is the essence of the economics of education approach.

Even so, a question or two can be raised. The authors say:

> If it is difficult to estimate the social and private benefits of postsecondary education in general, it is probably even tougher to do so at a more detailed level...[And] substantial fee differentials would likely result in significant logistical problems, such as how to allocate money to faculties (or departments?) according to the principles underlying the pricing scheme.

This statement reflects a particular perspective concerning the structure of student charges in the presence of government subsidies. In particular, it implies that if research cannot sort out the externalities in higher education, the charges should be made fairly similar. The implicit assumption is that the externalities differ significantly across courses of study and, indeed, are higher in high-cost courses.

A preferable and practical approach for policy is to argue that charging for higher education is essentially about cost recovery. That is, given that taxpayers in general, in Canada and many other countries, pay an important part of the cost of university services, a reasonable method of making a system more economically sensible is to assume that the externalities are constant across graduates in different areas (and who could establish otherwise?) and to base the charge on proportional cost recovery. Because course-cost data are available, this approach would be easy to implement.

In other words, one can argue that the fee should attempt not to reflect the externalities by course, but instead to diminish the typical taxpayer's obligation for the costs. This was the goal of the committee that recommended the HECS system in Australia, but the government chose instead to adopt a uniform charge regime. Canadian policymakers should note that cost-determined charges are the preferred arrangements of all academic commentators on HECS.

If externalities were easy to compute and understand, the decision about course-related differentials would obviously be different, but the fact is that economists are not able to estimate the spillovers from higher education. The cost-recovery approach is easily defensible but is surprisingly not one supported strongly in Finnie and Schwartz.

On this issue too, the authors note that differential fees have the potential to limit the access of the poor to some of the more expensive (and lucrative) courses, such as medicine. Insofar as this comment implies that differential charges by course are inappropriate, it is a narrow view of payment options, reflecting the nature of Canadian student loans, rather than what might be possible in a better system. For example, it would not be hard to design an ICR program with significant differences in course costs that also does not affect the access of the poor to the system.

The Old CSLP

Finnie and Schwartz's sections on the CSLP that used to be in place (the Old CSLP) and the criticisms that led to its revision raise some interesting points.

The Eligibility Rules

First, as a non-Canadian, I find the description of the Old CSLP less accessible than it might have been. Much of one's view of the efficacy of a loans system lies in the detail of the eligibility rules, what they mean for coverage, and thus the potential access of the less advantaged. It matters to know the size of loans in the context of the rate at which the assistance abates with family income, at what level of family income this abatement begins, and how the means-testing rules relate to the average and distribution of the country's family incomes. Presumably, the authors omitted this information because of interprovincial differences in the rules; nevertheless, an example or two would have allowed some perspective.

Poor Targeting

Of the several problems with the Old CSLP that the authors point to, poor targeting of the loans (in that some students got too little and others too much) is a common characteristic of student financing and related social security policy. The only real solution is somehow to devise arrangements that put the onus of the decision on the unit that best knows financial needs, the individual student. This was the fundamental motivation for the AUSTUDY Loans Supplement described earlier.

Default

Finnie and Schwartz also discuss the issue of default, one of the most significant problems of traditional loans schemes. Although some of the rules of the Old CSLP probably added to the frequency of default, the authors do not directly raise the biggest issue as a criticism of Canadian approaches. Instead, they consider it later in their discussion of ICR, but its significance is worth highlighting now.

As the authors acknowledge, one of the great advantages of ICR — and by implication one of the great disadvantages of Canadian approaches — is that the mechanism offers students protection from the possibility of not being able to repay their loan obligations in the future because of a lack of resources. The CSLP, old and new, misses the essential issue of providing default protection for prospective students who want to borrow.

This point is worth exploring from the conceptual basis of market failure in the area of human capital financing. What is usually raised in this context is that banks will not offer loans for educational investments unless there is some form of guaranteed repayment. The financial institutions take this position essentially because such loans involve no natural salable collateral, as there is, for example, in lending for the purchase of a house.

While this fact provides justification for government intervention in the form of guaranteeing loan repayments to banks, it does not address the other market failure in student loan financing: that risk-averse or poor prospective students may shy away from borrowing because they are overly concerned about not being able to repay. Having to default would affect their credit reputation and access to other loans, such as for a house.[5]

Mortgage-style loans cannot take away the possibility of default with its potential for bankruptcy and the loss of a credit reputation. Thus, such loan arrangements are apt to discourage enrollments by the excessively risk averse and by those who are from poor backgrounds and thus less likely to be in a position to cover the repayment when it is required. Although Finnie and Schwartz recognize this issue, they do not, in the opinion of this ICR supporter, promote it enough as a criticism of the Canadian arrangements. The CSLP will not be getting it right until this problem is fixed.

The Empirical Analysis

For academics, this chapter is potentially the most important contribution of the study. Good data and sensible research are rare in most areas of student finances, and this part of the analysis has both.

It would have been even better if a clearer framework had motivated the empirical work. While reading this chapter, I kept asking myself, what exactly are the authors interested in showing? and is there a thesis that will be informed by the detailed and careful statistical descriptions being explored?

Most obviously, what do the results show as indicators of the strengths and weaknesses of the Old versus the New CSLP? Of the

---

5 One only has to take a look at the new posters designed to encourage students repay student loans to be convinced that the protection of one's credit reputation is a significant issue.

potential strengths of the New CSLP? What do they mean for the question of whether or not there should be a completely different way of doing this?

New information is useful, and the Finnie and Schwartz data have presentational and statistical strengths, in part because the numbers are hard to come by in international terms. But what is needed here is greater attention to what the relationships uncovered mean for the fundamental debate about the right way to organize Canadian student finances. The bottom line for policy of the empirical research is unfortunately not clear.

ICR Student Loan Schemes

For this particular reviewer, the chapter on ICR schemes is the most interesting part of the work. In general Finnie and Schwartz do an excellent job in explaining the advantages of ICR. It is therefore somewhat surprising that they are not more critical of the CSLP's lack of sensitivity to the future income of students.

One of the less strong aspects of the analysis is the lack of attention to international experience with ICR, particularly in Australia, which has had such a scheme in operation since 1989, and New Zealand, which has had one since 1992. From the Australian experience, there are now considerable data addressing some of the concerns Finnie and Schwartz express. These concerns include the following:

- The government would have to find considerable loan resources in the short term to cover the fees, even if they would be paid back later.
- There would be substantial uncertainty about the financing body's ability to recover the repayments.
- If the system were unsubsidized and not mandatory, there would be potential for adverse selection in that those who expect high-cost funding from the ICR might choose other methods of financing, leaving in the pool those least likely to pay in full.

On the first issue, it is disappointing that the authors did not reference Barr's important book (1976), given that he seems to have found a private sector financing solution for ICR in the United Kingdom. He suggests using private banks for loans and having the government guarantee to repay a significant proportion of the outlays while collecting repayments through the tax system or its equivalent.[6]

In Australia, HECS raised revenue immediately because some students chose to pay their higher education charge on enrollment (This possibility of obtaining some funds rapidly was a reason the up-front payment option was introduced.) Clearly, there is scope for minimizing initial outlays from the change to an ICR. Finnie and Schwartz needed to consider options useful in the Canadian context.

The second problem, uncertainty concerning the repayment streams, seems relatively easy to fix. When Australia introduced its version of ICR, cross-sectional average income profiles by education, sex, and age were employed to estimate what might happen. Not long after, microsimulation modeling[7] was used to produce more sophisticated revenue projections. The different techniques came up with broadly similar results and seem so far to be predicting well.

The cross-sectional labor market data available in Canada are sufficiently sophisticated to allow similar predictions (indeed, I have used Canadian data to make this point). Moreover, Canada is a world leader in microsimulation modeling,[8] with Statistics Canada distributing relevant information. Clearly, finding out about the likely future revenue from a Canadian ICR would not be a difficult task.

The relevance of the third matter, adverse selection, depends on the rules of an ICR scheme. To illustrate that the issue can be avoided, again take the Australian example and put it into the Canadian context. A compulsory charge to be paid to the government when

---

6 This is in essence how the Australian AUSTUDY Loans Supplement works.

7 Microsimulation is the best available approach to estimating future government revenue, basically because it takes into account the many possible different experiences of individual students (see Harding 1994).

8 For an application using Canadian data, see Wolfson (1989).

and only if future income is at a particular level could be implemented on top of current Canadian fees. No adverse selection in the
choice of financing would be possible because no borrowing would
be required to satisfy the obligation. And with a discount for up-front
payment, the government would receive revenue instantly.

All of the other arguments against ICR mentioned by Finnie
and Schwartz are issues related to design parameters. There will
always be worries about whether or not there will be labor market
disincentive effects, that some people might face very long periods
of repayment, and that some people might behave in ways that avoid
repayment. Of course these issues exist, but they are not problems
of ICR *per se*. They are general matters for all student loan program
arrangements and can be avoided or exacerbated by the nature of
the system.

From all this, the case offered against ICR is weak. The basic
story seems then to be that it is not difficult to believe that with more
imagination and understanding of international approaches to ICR,
such a system could be made to work in Canada. That the authors
later suggest a pilot program implies that their thinking is probably
not too far from mine.

The New CSLP
and the Conclusion

Finnie and Schwartz endorse several of the changes reflected in the
New CSLP: increases in consistency between provinces in the eligibility rules; the payment of a flat 5 percent premium to banks to
compensate them for the default insurance transferred from the
government; the fact that banks' being now wholly responsible for
default coverage may lead to more flexible contracts between them
and students; and the extension of interest relief beyond the unemployed to borrowers in jobs with low earnings.

For those of us not fully cognizant of the nature and possible
impact of these changes in the CSLP, more detail is necessary. Moreover, the authors do not make enough of an attempt to relate the

alleged improvements in the CSLP to the essence of the economics of education.

It may be useful for this ICR supporter to comment briefly on the issue of collection costs. For a government to pay the banks a 5 percent loading to cover all collection costs seems clearly to be an improvement over the Old CSLP, but how much would it cost to have an ICR run through the existing tax collection system? Again, reference to the Australian experience is instructive.

Australia uses the central tax collection agency, the Australian Tax Office, for the collection of higher education charges. Its cost of administration is about $5.5 million per year,[9] which is 1.3 percent of the revenue collected (currently about $400 million annually). That percentage is clearly a lot smaller than 5 percent, although, to be fair, the higher education institutions have had small increased administration costs. But the bottom line is that if ICR is the way ahead, it can be designed to be administratively efficient.

Conclusion

The best single idea in the Finnie and Schwartz study lies in the suggestion of an ICR pilot program for Canada. One can only wait to see if this suggestion is taken up, but the case for it seems incontrovertible. If the political forces are not convinced that a fundamental move away from the conventional student financing approaches is in order, having evidence of the effects and administrative challenges of a potentially better system is critical.

The most important single omission in the study is its lack of recognition of the significance of means testing (indeed, of eligibility rules generally) in the availability of Canadian student loans. My recent speaking engagements at two Canadian forums on ICR[10] were

9 Information from correspondence with the Australian Tax Office.

10 Both organized by Alan Harrison of the Economics Department at McMaster University, Hamilton.

met by a cacophony of protest from student groups. The reason is easily understandable.

Canadian student loans are available only to those who meet the eligibility criteria, which cut out a very large number of students. Thus, if fees are increased because ICR is an easier (that is, default-protected) method of repayment, a great many students will face higher charges with no compensation. This issue can be avoided if the charge system is universal with eligibility not defined by family income.

The point is significant when the issue of intrafamily sharing of financial resources is raised. If family income is the defining criterion for eligibility, some apparently advantaged individuals may be cut out of the system because their parents or partners will not share equitably or just do not agree with the value the prospective student accords education. Means testing on the basis of family income entrenches this problem, but an ICR designed around the individual's future ability to pay avoids the issue.

A data issue follows from the concerns related to means testing. If there is a lack of intrafamily sharing of resources for higher education, those affected may not be observed because they have not enrolled. In other words, the authors can never be sure that the CSLP has been a success unless the data sample includes those not attending higher education, as well as students and former students. It follows that caution is necessary given the samples used.[11]

Notwithstanding the criticisms noted above, Finnie and Schwartz have made a valuable contribution to the Canadian and international debate related to higher education student financing. It matters that there is an up-to-date and accessible treatment of changes to the CSLP and their potential implications. The study will further clarify what are good and what are poor loan systems, and thus, one hopes, encourage further productive reform.

---

11 Assessments of the impact of the introduction of the Australian ICR sampled both students and groups that could have enrolled but chose not to. The scheme had no identifiable impact on either total demand for or the access of the poor to higher education (Chapman 1996).

References

Barr, Nicholas. 1976. *Student Loans: The Next Steps*. Aberdeen: Aberdeen University Press.

Chapman, Bruce. 1992. *AUSTUDY: Towards a More Flexible System*. Canberra: Australian Government Printing Service.

———. 1996. "Conceptual Issues and the Australian Experience with Income Contingent Charges for Higher Education." Centre for Economic Policy Research, Australian National University. Mimeographed.

Harding, Ann. 1994. "Financing Higher Education: An Assessment of Income Contingent Loan Options and Repayment Patterns Over the Life Cycle." Paper presented to the 23rd Conference of Australian Economists, Gold Coast, Queensland.

Wolfson, M. 1989. "Divorce, Home Maker Pensions and Life Cycle Analysis." *Population Policy and Review* 8: 25–54.

Student Loans and the Knowledge-Based Economy

Paul Davenport

Finnie and Schwartz's monograph on student loans in Canada could not have come at a better time. In all ten provinces, tuition fees have been increasing in recent years, both in absolute terms and as a percentage of total postsecondary expenditures. At the same time, grants to postsecondary institutions have been cut in most provinces, as both the federal and provincial levels of government seek to reduce or eliminate persistent budgetary deficits. There is every indication that these trends of tuition increases and grant restraint will continue into the future. Throughout Canada, there is a growing anxiety among students, parents, and postsecondary institutions that higher fees will soon cut off access to higher education for a growing number of potential students.

In this context, the technical analysis of Finnie and Schwartz helps shed light on two key issues facing Canadians: What amount of student debt is reasonable, given the higher average earnings of postsecondary graduates? Will Canadian governments, federal and provincial, have the financial resources and political will to fund loan systems that ensure that financial need is not a barrier to qualified students who seek access to postsecondary education?

These issues have high stakes for Canada, involving its future prosperity in a competitive global economy based increasingly on knowledge. In his superb book *Post-Capitalist Society*, Peter Drucker (1993) argues that, during the latter part of the twentieth century, human economy is undergoing a fundamental change in which the scarce resource is knowledge, rather than, as in previous epochs, land, labor, or physical or financial capital. The economic leaders of this society, as individuals and as firms, are those who can create, acquire, apply, and manage knowledge.

Within the knowledge-based economy, the health of Canada's postsecondary educational system is vital to all citizens. The graduates of that system have not simply improved their own opportunities; as a group, they represent, like university research, a significant social *investment* in the future growth and productivity of the country's economy as a whole. In their excellent review of the roles of research and technology in economic growth over the past century, David Mowery and Nathan Rosenberg (1989) emphasize that, because firms generally *cannot* buy new technology off the shelf, firms need in-house expertise to evaluate technological developments in their industries and to adapt them to local circumstances. Note that the argument here focuses not on the part of economic growth that theorists assign to human capital, but rather on the argument, put forward by Richard Nelson (1995), that increases in education and human capital are vital to the *entire* process of economic growth, including advances in technology and capital intensity. In the knowledge-based economy, productivity growth requires the development and effective use of new technologies, advances that in turn depend on the number and quality of postsecondary graduates who serve as the knowledge workers Drucker describes.

It is this broader context that gives such importance to the work of Finnie and Schwartz. Their contribution centers on three areas: a description of the evolution of the Canada Student Loans Program (CSLP); an analysis of student debt and repayment; and a discussion of income contingent repayment (ICR) loan programs and the appropriate level of tuition fees.

The Development of the CSLP

From 1964 to 1995, the CSLP guaranteed loans made to students by private institutions (generally banks) and paid the interest on those loans while the borrowers were in school. By 1993, 2.2 million students had borrowed $9.6 billion. The government had taken over about 20 percent of the loans from the lending institution; of these, the secretary of state reported in 1993, one-third had been collected, one-third seemed "potentially collectible," and one-third were written off as uncollectible, for an ultimate default rate of some 7 percent. The major conclusion of Finnie and Schwartz is that the federal guarantee provided the banks with little incentive to expend real resources in collecting loans in arrears, resulting in a need for government to coordinate much of the collection, at high cost.

In August 1995, the federal government announced a new CSLP approach designed to eliminate this incentive problem. Under the redesigned program, the private lending institutions have become fully responsible for collection and defaults in return for a full payment of 5 percent of the loans that enter the repayment phase each year. This change is expected to have three beneficial effects: the federal government's costs for loans that come due are fixed at 5 percent, and it has no liability for defaults; banks can offer more flexible repayment terms; and the banks have a greater incentive to collect loans in arrears. The latter two factors should lead to a reduction in defaults.

Student Debt and Repayment

Finnie and Schwartz present a wealth of data based on the National Graduates Surveys of Statistics Canada, which interviewed some 16,000 university graduates and 8,000 college graduates from each of the classes of 1982, 1986, and 1990 two and five years after graduation. The authors focus on the incidence and amount of borrowing among these former students, the proportion of loans repaid after two years, and the percentage of graduates who experienced difficulties in repayment.

I want to summarize a small part of the data: that concerned with those who graduated with a bachelor's degree in 1990. Of the 1990 bachelor's graduates, 54 percent did not undertake government-backed loans; the remaining 46 percent borrowed an average of $8,700. Those who borrowed had a debt-to-earnings ratio of 0.30 and repaid 47 percent of their debts during their first two years after graduation. Only 16 percent of the borrowers had failed to pay at least 15 percent of those debt during those two years after graduation. Although some students reported difficulties in repaying the loans, largely because of unemployment or insufficient earnings from work, the authors point out that these were a small minority of all bachelor's graduates.

Using computations based on figures in the text, I compiled Table 1, which is a summary of the class of 1990. In my view, these number reflect a student loan system that is working well, one in which most students can be expected to pay back their loans over a reasonable period. That view is confirmed by the overall 7 percent default rate for CSLP loans referred to above. (Indeed, 7 percent overstates the default rate for graduates of universities and provincially funded colleges; the authors cite the auditor-general of Canada, who noted in 1990 that students from private trade schools made up a disproportionate share of the defaults.)

Tuition Levels and Quality

I do disagree with Finnie and Schwartz on two points of presentation: the debate about tuitions that vary across academic programs, and the recounting of what the Organisation for Economic Cooperation and Development (OECD) said recently about Canadian education.

In an otherwise excellent discussion of tuition levels (Appendix B), the authors seem unable to take a clear position on the desirability of varying fees by program and indeed appear attracted to the arguments against such variation. I find the case for fee variation by program to be overwhelming (Davenport 1996). In many provinces, government controls on fees over the past two decades have required universities to charge nearly identical fees for programs such as those in the humanities and in the health profes-

Table 1:   *1990 Bachelor's Graduates:*
            Loan Status in 1992

	Percent of Total
Did not have a government-back loan	54
Had fully repaid their loans after two years	12
Had loans outstanding but did not report difficulties	27
Had loans outstanding and reported difficulties	7
Total	*100*

Source: My computations from data in Finnie and Schwartz. The figures here are rounded
         simple averages of the male and female data given.

sions, even though the latter may cost many times more per student and afford much higher earnings expectations.

This case is one in which efficiency and equity point in the same direction: universities should be allowed to charge more tuition to students in programs with high earnings expectations and high program costs, and loan systems should adjust accordingly. Finnie and Schwartz find that, of former students with debt remaining after two years after graduation, the percentage experiencing difficulties in repayment was 34 percent among those who had studied fine arts and humanities and 8 percent among those who had taken medical and health sciences. Surely postsecondary institutions should charge more for degrees in medicine than in poetry when medical students have much higher expected earnings and their program is much more costly to provide.

My second quibble concerns the conclusion to the monograph, in which the authors cite the OECD (1992) on the high percentage of gross domestic product that Canada spends on postsecondary education. They then say:

At the same time, the OECD analysts judged the performance of the system less than commensurably superior; one of the reports concludes, "Canada spends a lot on education, but does not seem to be getting good value for money."

While the reader will conclude at this point that the OECD is criticizing *postsecondary* education in Canada, this is simply not the case. The OECD's discussion of education has indicators of quality only from the primary and secondary levels: weak basic skills in grade 8; students leaving high school without basic literacy and numeracy skills; poor ratings in international comparisons of math and science achievement during the final secondary year; and the lack of vocational courses in high school (ibid., 63–69). Moreover, all of the corrective actions suggested involve primary and secondary education (ibid., 76–77). With the exception of a reference to the distribution of apprenticeships, the report offers no criticism whatsoever of postsecondary education and for good reason — the Canadian university system is well known and well respected in most OECD countries.

Looking to the Future

I return now to the central theme of student debt. As the authors point out at several points, data from 1982 to 1990 on student debt and repayment should not make Canadians complacent about the future, in which tuition fees and debt levels will be significantly higher in proportion to expected earnings. They suggest that the CSLP take additional steps to help students experiencing difficulties in repayment: an extension of the existing interest relief provisions, consideration of a loan remission program for those above certain debt limits (such programs are in place in several provinces), and experimentation with an ICR plan with one or more of the provinces (Ontario has expressed interest in such a system). With ICR, repayment is tied to income, thereby allowing society to share the risk that individual students may have disappointing income experiences after graduation (see AUCC 1993). This risk sharing may be particularly important for students from low-income families, who may otherwise shy away from taking on the significant debt required for postsecondary education.

While these proposals strike me as reasonable, they need to be put in a clear overall fiscal and political context: the total cost of postsecondary loans in Canada is going to rise because of growing student numbers and rising tuition, and both the federal and provincial levels of government need to make a clear commitment to strengthening student loan systems. Making this point is vital at a time when governments across the country are cutting or capping expenditures in most programs: any arbitrary reduction or cap on government contributions to student loans inevitably will reduce access to postsecondary education. Above all, for the good reasons that Finnie and Schwartz give, Canadians must resist talk of their governments — federal or provincial — getting out of the loan business altogether and leaving students to arrange loans as individuals.

As A.W. Johnson (1985) pointed out over a decade ago, federal student loans are a *dual vehicle*: they help meet the needs of individual students, and they allow the federal government to participate in the core funding of universities and colleges. Federal participation is justified because of the importance of postsecondary education to *national* economic and social goals in the globally competitive, knowledge-based economy. Postsecondary student loans are an important national issue in the United States and a topic of debate during presidential and congressional elections because of their perceived importance for economic growth and innovation in the country as a whole. Since the loan issue should be no less important in Canada, Finnie and Schwartz deserve great credit for documenting the empirical and policy aspects of postsecondary student loans in the Canadian context.

References

Association of Universities and Colleges of Canada (AUCC). 1993. "A New Student Assistance Plan for Canada." A report by the AUCC Standing Advisory Committee on Funding. Ottawa.

Davenport, Paul. 1996. "Deregulation and Restructuring in Ontario's University System." *Canadian Business Economics* 4 (July-September): 27–36.

Drucker, Peter F. 1993. *Post-Capitalist Society*. New York: HarperCollins.

Johnson, A.W. 1985. *Giving Greater Point and Purpose to the Federal Financing of Post-Secondary Education and Research in Canada.* A report to the secretary of state. Ottawa: Secretary of State.

Mowery, David C., and Nathan Rosenberg. 1989. *Technology and the Pursuit of Economic Growth.* Cambridge: Cambridge University Press.

Nelson, Richard R. 1995. "The Agenda for Growth Theory: A Different Point of View." In *Modern Perspective on Economic Growth.* Ottawa: Canadian Institute for Advanced Research.

Organisation for Economic Co-operation and Development. 1992. *OECD Economic Surveys: Canada, 1992.* Paris: OECD.

Improvements to the Canada Student Loans Program:
Do Recent Changes Fit the Bill?

Harry Hassanwalia

The considerable current public debate about reforms to the educational system includes discussion of the access provided young Canadians as they strive to compete in a very tight market for jobs. The timely study by Ross Finnie and Saul Schwartz discusses many of the issues related to government-subsidized loans, providing some useful context for the unfolding public debate. It offers a rich body of empirical information on student loans and their repayment, as well as a review of the recent changes to the Canada Student Loans Program (CSLP).

The purpose of this comment is to provide a somewhat different assessment of these changes. Table 1 lists the main features of the "Old CSLP" and the "New CSLP," and, except for one point relating to the interest costs of class B loans, most of the details are virtually the same as Finnie and Schwartz describe. The benefits of some of the changes are, however, ambiguous at best.

High Losses in the Old CSLP

Any assessment of the changes to the Old CSLP requires a clear understanding of its problems and their sources. One weakness was the high level of losses. That the losses were high is undeniable, but unless the causes are correctly identified, it is doubtful that public policy will have the right solution.

Table 1:   ***Comparison of the***
Old CSLP and the New CSLP

	"Old" CSLP	"New" CLSP
Eligibility determined by:	Government	Government
Need assessment	Varied across provinces	More consistent across provinces
Maximum weekly limit	$105	$165
Credit risk taken by:	Government	Financial institution
Government compensation of financial institutions?	Full guarantee of principal	No guarantee but upfront fee of 5% of principal
Pricing of class A loans[a]	1–5-year government of Canada bond + 1%	Prime
Pricing of class B loans[a]	5–10-year government of Canada bond + 1%	Variable rate: capped at prime + 2.5%; fixed rate: capped at prime + 5.0%
Interest relief available for:	Up to 18 months	Up to 18 months
Repayment schedule	Fixed	Negotiable with financial institution
Default reported to credit bureaus?	No	Yes
Revenue Canada used to recover debt?	Yes[b]	No[c]

[a] See footnote 3 for explanation of class A and class B loans.

[b] The practice of using Revenue Canada to recover debts from refunds due was a recent change and was not in place for most of CSLP history.

[c] But, as explained in footnote 5, this practice may continue in a limited way even under the new CSLP.

As Table 1 shows, the New CSLP has three major innovations: (1) the risk is transferred to financial institutions, unlike the previous situation in which the government provided a full guarantee of the loans; (2) default can be reported to credit bureaus, affecting the borrower's credit rating; and (3) financial institutions have the discretion to set repayment terms in negotiation with the borrower, rather than having to use the previous fixed repayment schedules. These three innovations have been introduced in the expectation that they will, among other things, lower losses. To assess how effective they will be, however, it is important to attempt to determine the causes behind the losses. Below, I examine five potential causes and assess the effectiveness of the new CSLP against them.

Lack of Borrower Accountability

A student who borrowed under the Old CSLP could walk away from the loan and not have the default appear on his or her credit-rating files, a situation that is often blamed for the system's high losses. Indeed, it might have been one factor involved if there actually were many borrowers who reneged on their debts because it was costless to do so even though they were financially capable of servicing them. Save for anecdotal information, however, there is no substantive evidence to suggest this practice was widespread.

Moreover, even if there was abuse because of a lack of accountability under the old system, the situation would have changed in 1993 when the federal government started using Revenue Canada to recover debt, from income tax refunds due. This approach should have been quite effective in recovering most loans, except from borrowers facing outright financial hardship, and a substantial amount of recovery has, in fact, been made.[1]

In all other respects, financial institutions have no better credit-recovery powers than the government had. They are using collection agencies just as the government did. What additional benefit has the new process provided?

Lack of Government Expertise

Some people argue that, since the government is not in the business of credit-risk management, it likely did not have the expertise required to recover debt. This reasoning is not compelling. Given the small size of these loans, even the banks are using collection agencies. Moreover, the government had the powerful instrument of Revenue Canada to recover loans made under the Old CSLP. Again, what advantage does the New CSLP offer?

1 In the first two years of the change, $23 million and $18.7 million, respectively, were recovered (Canada 1996).

Financial Institutions' Lack of Incentive

Another claim is that, even though financial institutions are in the business of credit-risk management, the design of the Old CSLP did not provide them sufficient incentives to improve debt recovery by working with potential defaulters, especially since doing so might have jeopardized their guarantees. This argument has some surface appeal, but even if financial institutions had incentives, they lacked the necessary tools.

Successful credit-risk management has four important tools: approving credit; pricing for risk; setting repayment schedules; and, in the case of impairment, taking appropriate steps to maximize recoveries. Under the old CSLP, financial institutions could not determine the price, the amount of the loan, or the repayment terms. The new system may give them more incentives, but the tools available to them will remain limited. They cannot limit the amount of borrowing based on assessments of students' ability to repay since the government determines eligibility and the amount of borrowing. Neither can they price the loans commensurate with the risk since the government caps the rate. The point is that a loan under either the Old or the New CSLP lacks some of the features of a standard credit instrument.

Moreover, as Finnie and Schwartz suggest, the old CSLP was not a profitable business for financial institutions. The reason was the prescribed interest rate. Even if the 1 percent provided for administrative costs had fully covered the expenses an institution incurred in running the program, it would have averaged a loss on these loans. The marginal cost of funds for financial institutions is higher than the interest rate on government securities. Since the rate on these loans was set for one year at a time, the relevant marginal cost for a financial institution was the one-year cost of funds, which would generally be higher than the one-year government bond rate.[2]

---

2 The marginal cost of funds for banks is the interest rate paid or earned by them for borrowing or lending funds in money markets from or to other similarly rated corporations. Since government has a better rating than any private corporation,...

Presumably to ameliorate this potential loss, the government bonds used to calculated the prescribed rate had terms longer than one year (according to Finnie and Schwartz, one to five years for the class A loans and five to ten years for class B). Then, a necessary (though not sufficient) condition for earning a positive spread was that the yield curve be positively sloped beyond one year. In fact, for most of the years from 1982 to 1990, the yield curve from one to ten years was negatively sloped or flat (see Table 2).[3] That negative slope resulted from the tight monetary policy used throughout this period to combat high inflation.

Recall that these years were an extraordinary period of monetary tightness. Today, the yield curve is back to its normal upward slope. Moreover, the New CSLP's higher caps on the interest rates financial institutions can charge may improve the financial situation they face (as long as the riskiness of the loans does not rise).

Economic Factors

By far the most compelling reason for loan losses seems to have been economic conditions. Much evidence suggests that job prospects for Canadian youth have deteriorated from what they were for previous generations (see, for example, Little 1996). Finnie and Schwartz reflect this situation empirically when they find that having insufficient earnings was one of the main reasons for graduates' being unable to repay government-subsidized loans. Their examination of three student cohorts that graduated in 1982, 1986, and 1990, respectively, with loans outstanding shows that debt-to-earnings ratios

---

Note 2 - cont'd.

including a bank, the marginal cost of funds for banks would be higher than the interest rate paid by government. Financial institutions do, of course, often invest in government bonds that do not cover their marginal cost of funds, but they do so for purposes of liquidity or interest rate risk management. Further, investment in government bonds does not generate the administrative costs of a student loan.

3 While the student is in school and the government is paying the interest, loan is classified as class A. Once the borrower leaves school and responsibility for payment of interest shifts to him or her, the loan is classified as class B. Under the old CSLP, class B loans were guaranteed by the government.

Table 2:   ***Difference between Yields on Government***
of Canada Bonds with Various Terms

	2 year – 1 year	3 year – 1 year	5 year – 1 year	10 year – 1 year
	(basis points)			
1982	– 110	– 102	– 73	– 32
1983	46	51	108	180
1984	– 6	7	41	94
1985	16	29	51	89
1986	– 20	– 31	– 25	– 10
1987	12	15	26	51
1988	– 39	– 43	– 41	– 17
1989	– 117	– 160	– 185	– 200
1990	– 113	– 138	– 156	– 177
Average difference	– 37	– 41	– 28	– 2

Source: Annual averages calculated from interest rates published by the Bank of Canada.

generally rose consistently, implying ever-greater hardships for recent graduates. Given this result, it seems evident that successive
cohorts of graduating students have faced poorer earnings prospects
relative to the debt they have had to incur.

Moreover, debt-to-earnings ratios do not fully reflect debt burdens in an environment of interest rate changes.[4] For example, a
30 percent debt-to-income ratio with the interest rate at 10 percent
implies an interest payment burden similar to that of a 60 percent
debt-to-income ratio with the interest rate at 5 percent. For much of
the period covered by Finnie and Schwartz, interest rates were
changing, so the debt-servicing ratio (principal and interest payments as a ratio of earnings) is a more meaningful measure than the
debt-to-earnings ratio. Table 3 shows the debt-servicing ratios con-

4 Finnie and Schwartz also note that the debt-to-earnings ratio may be misleading
  in the sense that it ignores the absolute size of earnings. Sparing a certain
  proportion of income for debt servicing may be more difficult for a low-income
  debtor than for one with a higher income. This point is valid and extends to the
  debt-servicing ratios I have calculated in Tables 3 and 4.

sistent with the debt-to-earnings ratios shown in Finnie and Schwartz's Tables 6 and 7. Given the decline in interest rates from 1982 to 1986, the debt-servicing ratios show a less severe deterioration over this period than do the debt-to-earnings ratios. In contrast, the debt-servicing ratios show a greater deterioration from 1986 to 1990 than the authors find for debt-to-earnings ratios, mainly because interest rates increased during this period.

Lack of Flexibility in Payments

Under the Old CSLP, loans had to be repaid on a ten-year amortization schedule, and if a borrower encountered difficulty in repayment, the financial institution had no incentive to reschedule repayments; it simply asked the federal government to exercise its guarantee. Some people suggest that financial institutions' lack of flexibility may have exacerbated the difficulties with repayments.

Yet, alternative interpretations are possible. If rescheduling repayments was the best way to minimize losses, that strategy would have been the rational choice for the government once it had exercised its guarantee. So even if the guarantee left financial institutions no incentive to be flexible, the same cannot be said of the government.

One can also question the extent to which greater flexibility in loan repayment might have ameliorated borrowers' hardship. Table 4 shows the interest burden component alone for the cohorts and classifications covered in Table 3 and in Finnie and Schwartz's Tables 6 and 7. Effectively, this burden is what an average borrower would have had to carry if he or she did not have to make any principal payments at all, an extreme form of repayment flexibility. A comparison of Tables 3 and 4 confirms, as expected, that, for each cohort, the burden would have declined significantly from what it actually faced. Even with this flexibility, however, the burden for successive cohorts would have risen.

Moreover, a close examination of the two tables reveals another disturbing facet. Compare the full debt-servicing burden 1982 graduates faced (Table 3) with what the burden would have been for 1990 graduates had there been full deferment of principal repayment

(Table 4). Even if there had been the latter maximum flexibility, the hardship for many of the 1990 cohort would have been greater than for the 1982 cohort. In other words, a slower repayment schedule, while lowering the burden, would have not brought it down to the 1982 levels in aggregate.

An ancillary point is that, although the frozen borrowing limit is an important criticism of the Old CSLP, the financial situation could have been even worse if this limit had been raised.

In Summary

The point of all this is that, although there may have been many contributory factors, the difficulties in repaying student loans seem to have reflected more fundamental economic forces — forces that the changes to the CSLP are unlikely to address.

Those changes seem to have been the result of some commonly held views about the causes of high losses, such as lack of accountability by the borrowers, lack of government expertise, and lack of flexibility. Not all these views can be factually corroborated. Of course, lack of incentives for financial institutions is probably relevant, but the new CSLP, while improving those incentives, does not provide the financial institutions with meaningful tools to effect recoveries.

The New CSLP

Even if the main problem for CSLP debt difficulties and losses is economic conditions, it is still useful to see if the new program has improved on some design features of the old one that may have contributed to higher-than-necessary losses. The clearest way to assess the changes is to raise a number of questions.

Will Greater Flexibility in Repayments Result?

Under the New CSLP, the financial institution and the borrower will negotiate the repayment schedule once the loan becomes class B (that

Table 3:   *Debt-Servicing-to-Income Ratios,*
              1982, 1986, and 1990

	Gender	1982	1986	% Change	1990	% Change
				(percent)		
Field of study (bachelor's graduates)						
Education	Male	3.7	4.6	24	6.0	31
	Female	3.9	5.1	30	6.0	18
Fine arts & humanities	Male	3.3	5.8	75	5.9	1
	Female	4.3	5.9	37	5.7	− 4
Commerce, economics, law	Male	2.7	4.5	66	5.3	19
	Female	3.7	4.6	24	5.7	23
Other social sciences	Male	3.1	5.1	65	5.7	11
	Female	3.9	6.1	55	6.7	10
Agriculture & biosciences	Male	2.5	4.5	79	5.5	23
	Female	4.3	4.5	3	5.5	23
Engineering	Male	2.5	3.3	33	3.7	13
	Female	—	1.8	—	4.4	144
Medical & health	Male	2.7	2.5	− 8	4.8	93
	Female	2.9	3.1	8	5.1	64
Maths & physical sciences	Male	3.1	3.3	6	3.7	13
	Female	3.9	3.8	− 3	4.4	17
Degree level						
College/CEGEP	Male	2.5	3.1	26	3.5	13
	Female	3.1	3.8	22	4.6	22
Bachelor's	Male	2.9	4.1	42	5.0	20
	Female	3.5	4.8	36	5.7	19
Master's	Male	2.7	3.0	10	3.4	13
	Female	3.1	2.8	− 10	4.3	52
PhD	Male	1.9	2.0	6	2.7	34
	Female	2.1	1.5	− 28	2.7	79

Note: I derived the debt-servicing ratios from Finnie and Schwartz's debt-to-income ratios using a ten-year amortization and interest rates of 15.99, 10.32, and 12.05 percent for 1982, 1986, and 1990, respectively. The interest rates were computed as 1 percent plus the six-month average (ending August of each year) for the five- to ten-year government of Canada bond rate.

Source: Author's calculations using data from Finnie and Schwartz, tables 6 and 7.

Table 4:   *Interest-Servicing-to-Income Ratios,*
1982, 1986, and 1990

	Gender	1982	1986	% Change	1990	% Change
				(percent)		
Field of study (bachelor's graduates)						
Education	Male	2.9	2.9	0	4.1	42
	Female	3.0	3.2	5	4.1	28
Fine arts & humanities	Male	2.6	3.6	41	4.0	10
	Female	3.4	3.7	11	3.9	4
Commerce, economics, law	Male	2.1	2.8	34	3.6	30
	Female	2.9	2.9	0	3.9	33
Other social sciences	Male	2.4	3.2	33	3.9	21
	Female	3.0	3.8	26	4.6	20
Agriculture & biosciences	Male	1.9	2.8	45	3.7	34
	Female	3.4	2.8	− 17	3.7	34
Engineering	Male	1.9	2.1	8	2.5	23
	Female	—	1.1	—	3.0	165
Medical & health	Male	2.1	1.5	− 26	3.3	110
	Female	2.2	2.0	− 12	3.5	78
Maths & physical sciences	Male	2.4	2.1	− 14	2.5	23
	Female	3.0	2.4	− 22	3.0	27
Degree level						
College/CEGEP	Male	1.9	2.0	2	2.4	23
	Female	2.4	2.4	− 1	3.1	32
Bachelor's	Male	2.2	2.6	15	3.4	31
	Female	2.7	3.0	10	3.9	29
Master's	Male	2.1	1.9	− 11	2.3	23
	Female	2.4	1.8	− 27	2.9	65
PhD	Male	1.4	1.2	− 14	1.8	46
	Female	1.6	0.9	− 42	1.8	95

Note: I derived the debt-servicing ratios from Finnie and Schwartz's debt-to-income ratios using a ten-year amortization and interest rates of 15.99, 10.32, and 12.05 percent for 1982, 1986, and 1990, respectively. The interest rates were computed as 1 percent plus the six-month average (ending August of each year) for the five- to ten-year government of Canada bond rate.

Source: Author's calculations using data from Finnie and Schwartz, tables 6 and 7.

is, when the individual is no longer a student). Moreover, the financial institution has full flexibility in determining the approach to be taken when a loan becomes impaired. These two features seem to suggest that greater flexibility will be possible. But what is not clear is the extent to which financial institutions will take explicit account of the borrower's individual circumstances.

Finnie and Schwartz provide an interesting reading on the conflict that a financial institution is likely to face. In commenting on the weaknesses of the Old CSLP, they imply the desirability of flexibility in repayment schedules to take account of the former student's actual financial situation:

> CSLP loans had a maximum fixed payment period of ten years, *regardless of the actual size of the loan or the former student's financial situation* [emphasis added]. (11.)

Elsewhere, however, the authors caution that such flexibility could lead to inequitable treatment and favoritism:

> For example, students who seem more attractive as long-run clients might receive more favorable treatment than others, both when the loan is being taken out and, more important, during the repayment period when flexibility will be the relevant watchword. In particular, those whose parents or spouses are established clients and those with high earnings may receive preferential treatment....Thus, the risk of passing full management of collection over to the banks and opening up possibilities for efficiency and flexibility is that the door is similarly opened to inequitable treatment and favoritism. (74–75.)

These two comments combine to point out the likely course of action by financial institutions.

Private sector financial intermediaries are in the business of managing credit risk and so should be better than government at doing it. Yet, as noted before, of the four important tools for successful credit-risk management — approving credit; pricing for risk; setting repayment schedules; and, in case of impairment, taking appropriate steps to maximize recoveries — the New CSLP restricts the use of both approving credit and pricing.

The only tools financial institutions have left for efficient credit-risk management are the repayment schedule and changes to it in case of impairment. But what factors can they use in determining whether the best loss-minimization strategy in the face of an impairment is slower repayment or quick recovery? Two factors that clearly seem to matter are the individual's family situation and his or her future earning potential given the field of study completed. But if institutions consider such factors, Finnie and Schwartz suggest, they might be engaging in undesirable behavior leading to "inequitable treatment and favoritism." So, on the one hand there is a perception that financial institutions should be more flexible, but on the other the individual borrowers' specific circumstances — the factors on which banks might base flexible decisions — could be perceived as discriminatory.

Given this conflict, the most likely outcome is that financial institutions will be extremely limited in their flexibility in order to avoid perceptions of discrimination. They will likely opt for the low-risk approach of avoiding any case-by-case exceptions and instead rely on objective, formula-based policies.

Will Default Rates Fall?

Under the Old CSLP, defaulting on a student loan did not affect an individual's credit rating because reporting to credit bureaus was not permitted. The New CSLP does permit such reporting, so a default will have an impact on the credit rating. This change may work toward lowering default rates. On the other hand, the removal of the use of Revenue Canada in effecting recoveries may offset any net improvement.[5]

---

5 The use of Revenue Canada may still occur to some very small extent. Banks may sell 3 percent of their class B loans created in a year back to the government at 5 percent of their face value, and the government may then use whatever means it has, including Revenue Canada, to recover the loan. Of the recoveries, 75 percent net of the buyback price will go to lenders.

Overall, the fact that recovery is now the responsibility of the financial institution should neither increase nor decrease loss potential. (As I suggested before, if the rational choice for maximizing recoveries under the old system had been to make flexible arrangements for repayment, the government could have done so once it took over impaired loans.)

In fact, default rates may rise, because of higher borrowing limits and because the interest rate will be higher than in the past.[6] Both factors will raise debt-servicing costs.

Will Efficient Risk Pooling Result?

Without government subsidy, financial institutions would price credit commensurate with risk, and students at the low end of the credit-risk scale would face a price likely to dissuade them from borrowing. The presence of the government subsidy enables financial institutions to lower the price of risk, so they can underprice the loan by this amount. The loan eligibility requirements of government are, however, based on need assessments that implicitly take in everyone who falls below a certain credit risk; within that class, there is no further risk tiering. So students who have identical needs but are pursuing different programs of study with different employment prospects and so different risk are all pooled together and pay the same price — a form of cross-subsidization from those of better credit risk to those of weaker credit risk. It is not clear whether this approach can be termed "efficient" risk pooling, as Finnie and Schwartz imply. Efficiency requires the pooling of similar classes of risks (that is, risks drawn from a population with a similar probability distribution and expected losses), but where the law of large numbers permits that, on the average credit experience equals the expected credit experience.

---

6 Although, as Finnie and Schwartz suggest, class B loans will still likely attract below-market rates of interest for the risk, the level of rates for student loans relative to the general level of interest rates will be higher than the proportion under the Old CSLP.

Does the CSLP Help Banks' Business Development?

Finnie and Schwartz suggest that, for a financial institution, the full value of being in the student loan business is not just the expected rate of return on the loans but also the value of the future business that might be won by attracting and keeping student borrowers.

This hypothesis may overstate the merits of relationship banking. Given the competitive Canadian financial market and the rising level of public sophistication, customers generally choose a financial institution on the basis of convenience of access, quality of service, price, and product choice, not on whether they have banked with that institution at some time in their lives.

Do Other Approaches Exist?

The New CSLP should be treated as one among many different approaches that are emerging. As Finnie and Schwartz conclude, there is merit in examining income contingent repayment (ICR) strategies. One example is Ontario's recently announced plan to test an ICR scheme for its student loans program (Lewington 1996). Recently, too, the University of Toronto announced that, for selected education programs, graduates who choose below-average-paying positions will receive its assistance in paying off part of their loans during the first five years after graduation (ibid.). Yet another example is the privatized MBA program in science and technology offered at Queen's University, which exempts graduates from interest payments on their loans until they obtain a job that pays at least $50,000 a year (DeGroot 1996).[7] (Of course, ICR programs are not necessarily

---

7 The Queen's program involves no public subsidization of tuition fees. Rather, it entails the student's taking a loan for 100 percent of tuition fees plus up to an additional $10,000 living expenses from a bank under an arrangement with the university. While the student is in school, the university pays the interest on the full amount of the loan. On graduation, the borrower takes over servicing the loan related to living expenses, but the university continues to pay interest on the tuition portion of the loan until the individual obtains employment with a salary of $50,000 a year. Once the graduate reaches that threshold of salary, the interest and principal become his or her responsibility. The moral hazard implicit...

free from problems such as moral hazard and potential cross-sub-sidization from better-salaried students, though the programs at Queen's and the University of Toronto would seem to be similar to a warranty provided by any supplier of a good or service.) One issue that does not seem to be getting adequate attention is that financial assistance is a government, not private sector, responsibility, so that if there is any residual or final risk in any of these programs, it must reside with government.

Overall Assessment

The New CSLP is a revised system that increases funding to students but at a higher effective cost than in the past. Borrowers who experience weak earnings or lack of employment will not be any better off. They may encounter more flexibility from financial institutions in repayment, but their interest rate will be higher than in the past and nonperformance will impose a cost on them in terms of poor credit ratings. The previous arrangements under which the government was able to use Revenue Canada to recover debt from tax refunds seemed to have an implicit ICR option (because a refund generally accrues only if an individual had had enough income in the first place). This feature will not be significant in the new approach.

Thus, the only clear benefit in the new system seems to be increased consistency in need-assessment procedures. This change did not require as much revamping of the total student loans system as has occurred.

Note 7 - cont'd.

...in any guarantee scheme and the potential for cross-subsidization are minimized through a number of measures, including eligibility requirements, entrance standards, and explicit agreements with the students that require them to actively look for employment and to disclose offers and salary. The program does, however, have a major weakness from the risk perspective of the bank. Should a borrower's lack of performance of his or her obligations result in the university's canceling its guarantee, the entire risk will fall on the bank.

Tuition Fees and Social/Private Benefits

An issue that emerges in any discussion of subsidization of post-secondary education is the setting of tuition fees, which leads directly to the subject of the social versus the private benefits of education. Although Finnie and Schwartz recognize the difficulties in reliable estimates of social benefits, they nonetheless suggest that the appropriate level for tuition fees is one-third of instruction costs, which implies that social benefits are some two-thirds of those costs. That various commissions investigating the mix of private and social benefits have recommended a similar level might be a reasonable argument but for the fact that other analysts find social benefits "amorphous" (West 1993, as cited by Finnie and Schwartz).

Although the social benefits of education are important, the measurement of these externalities is, in fact, unreliable. Therefore, it will always be difficult to justify one level of net subsidization relative to another. Measurement of private benefits may also be unreliable. Measurement of private benefits is unnecessary, however, if the system of tuition and subsidization is designed to recover a *substantial part* of the costs *ex post* on the basis of the explicit private benefit derived, which can be specified as income. This approach may not be the best solution, but it is preferable to a design in which arbitrary values are being assigned to public benefits. Ontario's proposed ICR plan, the University of Toronto's income-related loan subsidization, and Queen's University's job guarantees for MBAs are all programs effectively geared to cost recovery related to private benefits, although they are not necessarily adequate in terms of where eventual risk resides.

Conclusions

Finnie and Schwartz have provided a valuable and timely analysis that should encourage broader public debate about the educational system. I have, however, considerable uncertainty about the redesigned CSLP, and from which I do not expect such substantial benefits relative to the Old CSLP. It is fortunate that the new program is in place only for five years. At best, it should be considered an interim arrangement until more fundamental reforms are undertaken.

The most controversial aspect of the New CSLP is the transfer of the credit risk to financial institutions, while denying them the two most important tools of managing credit risk — pricing and determining eligibility. This design does not appear to promote an efficient partnership of government and the private sector. In any event, it is questionable whether any change was required to improve management of credit risk, when government had all the levers at its disposal. It is also questionable whether credit-risk management *per se* was the problem since the major reason for repayment problems seems to have been general economy-wide forces.

Perhaps policymakers and analysts need to look at broader issues, such as the potential match between the skills acquired through higher education and the skills needs of the economy. Those issues are, however, beyond the scope of the study and of this note.

References

Canada. 1996. *1996-97 Estimates, Part III, Expenditure Plan*. Ottawa: Supply and Services Canada.

DeGroot, P. 1996. "Good job is guaranteed at Queen's MBA program; innovative design unique among public sector universities." *The Edmonton Journal*, July 2, p. C3.

Lewington, J. 1996. "Students' payments, income to be tied — Ontario to test new loan scheme." *Globe and Mail* (Toronto), June 26, p. A1.

Little, Bruce. 1996. "Gaining at working growing harder." *Globe and Mail* (Toronto), July 12, p. A1.

West, Edwin. 1993. *Ending the Squeeze on Universities*. Montreal: Institute for Research on Public Policy.

The Contributors

Bruce Chapman is Professor of Economics and Director of the Centre for Economic Policy Research at the Australian National University, Canberra. He is a labor economist, educated at Yale University, and has published about a hundred articles in journals and books. As a consultant to the Australian government, he helped design an income contingent charge system for that country in 1988, and since that time he has given a large number of presentations in other countries on the Australian system.

Paul Davenport is President and Vice-Chancellor of the University of Western Ontario. He graduated "with great distinction" from Stanford University in 1969 with a BA (Honors Economics), and then received MA and PhD degrees from the University of Toronto. Dr. Davenport's research in economics has centered on the theory of economic growth, analysis of the productivity slowdown in Canada over the past two decades, and federal-provincial fiscal arrangements. He has published widely in these fields in academic journals and books. Dr. Davenport is also a public advocate of the values of higher education, with a particular commitment to maintaining excellence in university teaching and research. He strongly believes that academic priorities should determine budgetary allocations and that universities should invest selectively in areas of quality and distinction.

Ross Finnie was educated at Queen's University, the London School of Economics, and the University of Wisconsin-Madison. He is currently a Visiting Professor in the School of Public Administration at Carleton University and a Visiting Scholar at Statistics Canada. His current work includes a study of the school-to-work transition of recent Canadian postsecondary graduates using the national Graduates Surveys on which the empirical work reported in this book is based. A second major line of research focuses on the income dynamics of Canadians using longitudinally linked tax files of Canadian families.

Harry Hassanwalia has an MBA (Financial Economics) from Concordia University, where he also pursued postgraduate studies in Economics. He joined the Royal Bank of Canada's Economics Department in 1983, was appointed to the position of Assistant Chief Economist in 1986, and to the position of Deputy Chief Economist in 1996. He has had a broad range of responsibilities, with particular focus on financial institutions and the flow of funds in credit and capital markets.

Saul Schwartz has been a professor in the School of Public Administration at Carleton University since 1991. He received his PhD in Economics from the University of Wisconsin. His research interests focus on the impact of public policies on low-income individuals and families.

Members of the
C.D. Howe Institute[*]

The ARA Consulting Group Inc.
ARC Financial Corporation
Michael J. Adams
Alberta Energy Company Ltd.
Alcan Aluminium Limited
ATCO Ltd.
Avenor inc.
BC Gas Inc.
BC Sugar Refinery, Limited
BC TEL
BCE Inc.
BCE Mobile Communications Inc.
Bank of America Canada
Bank of Montreal
The Bank of Nova Scotia
Banque Laurentienne du Canada
Banque Nationale du Canada
Barrick Gold Corporation
Harry Baumann
Bayer Inc.
David Beatty
Bell Canada
Brent Belzberg
Roy F. Bennett
Beutel, Goodman & Company Ltd.
R.W. Billingsley
The Birks Family Foundation
The Bolt Supply House Ltd.
Bombardier Inc.
R.A.N. Bonnycastle
Gerald K. Bouey
Brascan Limited
M. David R. Brown
Pierre Brunet
Burns Fry Limited

Business Development Bank of Canada
CAE Inc.
CFCF Inc.
C.I. Mutual Funds Inc.
CIBC Wood Gundy Securities Inc.
The CRB Foundation
CT Financial
Robert C. Caldwell
The Calgary Chamber of Commerce
Camdev Corporation
Cameco Corporation
Canada Deposit Insurance Corporation
The Canada Life Assurance Company
Canada Overseas Investments Limited
Canada Post Corporation
Canadian Airlines International Ltd.
Canadian Association of Petroleum
  Producers
Canadian Bankers' Association
The Canadian Chamber of Commerce
Canadian Corporate Funding Ltd.
Canadian Federation of Independent
  Business
Canadian Hunter Exploration Ltd.
Canadian Imperial Bank of Commerce
Canadian Life and Health Insurance
  Association Inc.
Canadian National
Canadian Newspaper Association
Canadian Pacific Limited
Canadian Pulp & Paper Association
Canadian Utilities Limited
Cargill Limited
Chauvco Resources Ltd.
Ciba-Geigy Canada Ltd.

---

[*] The views expressed in this publication are those of the authors and do not necessarily reflect the opinions of the Institute's members.

Citibank Canada
Clairvest Group Inc.
Cogeco inc.
Consoltex Group Inc.
Consumers Gas
Coopers & Lybrand
Dr. Glen H. Copplestone
E. Kendall Cork
William J. Cosgrove
Co-Steel Inc.
Marcel Côté
Pierre Côté
John Crispo
Glen E. Cronkwright
John Crow
Crown Life Insurance Company Limited
Paul R. Curley
Thomas P. d'Aquino
Leo de Bever
W. Ross DeGeer
Catherine Delaney
Deloitte & Touche
Desjardins Ducharme Stein Monast
Robert Després
Deutsche Bank Canada
Iain St. C. Dobson
The Dominion of Canada General
    Insurance Company
DuPont Canada Inc.
The Eaton Foundation and The Eaton
    Group of Companies
Gordon H. Eberts
Edper Group Limited
Emerging Markets Advisors Inc.
The Empire Life Insurance Company
ENSIS Corporation
Ernst & Young
Export Development Corporation
Ronald J. Farano, Q.C.
Fidelity Investments Canada Limited
First Marathon Securities Limited
Aaron M. Fish
John P. Fisher
Fishery Products International Limited
C.J. Michael Flavell, Q.C.
Ford Motor Company of Canada, Limited
Formula Growth Limited

L. Yves Fortier, C.C., Q.C.
Four Seasons Hotels Limited
GSW Inc.
Jim Garrow
General Electric Canada Inc.
General Motors of Canada Limited
Joseph F. Gill
Gluskin Sheff + Associates Inc.
Goldman Sachs Canada
Goodman Phillips & Vineberg
Peter Goring
Dr. John A.G. Grant
Dr. Jerry Gray
The Great-West Life Assurance Company
Greyhound Lines of Canada
Morton Gross
Le Groupe Canam Manac
Groupe Sobeco Inc.
Dr. Geoffrey E. Hale
H. Anthony Hampson
C.M. Harding Foundation
G.R. Heffernan
Lawrence L. Herman
Hewlett-Packard (Canada) Ltd.
Gordon J. Homer
Honeywell Limited
Hongkong Bank of Canada
The Horsham Corporation
Dezsö Horváth
H. Douglas Hunter
Lou Hyndman, Q.C.
IBM Canada Ltd.
Imasco Limited
Imperial Oil Limited
Inco Limited
Inland Industrial Materials Limited
The Insurance Bureau of Canada
Interprovincial Pipe Line Inc.
Investment Dealers Association of Canada
The Investment Funds Institute of Canada
Investors Group Inc.
IPSCO Inc.
Tsutomu Iwasaki
The Jackman Foundation
The Jarislowsky Foundation
KPMG
Mark D. Kassirer

Koch Oil Co. Ltd.
Joseph Kruger II
Claude Lamoureux
R. John Lawrence
Jacques A. Lefebvre
Gérard Limoges
Loewen, Ondaatje, McCutcheon Limited
London Life Insurance Company
J.W. (Wes) MacAleer
McCallum Hill Companies
McCarthy Tétrault
W.A. Macdonald
Bruce M. McKay
McKinsey & Company
Maclab Enterprises
James Maclaren Industries Inc.
Jack M. MacLeod
McMillan Binch
MacMillan Bloedel Limited
William J. McNally
Mannville Oil & Gas Ltd.
Manulife Financial
Dr. Georg Marais
Marsh & McLennan Limited
Hon. Dwight N. Mason
Master Equity Investments Inc.
The Mercantile and General
    Reinsurance Group
William M. Mercer Limited
Merck Frosst Canada Inc.
Methanex Corporation
Metropolitan Life Insurance Company
Robert Mitchell Inc.
The Molson Companies Limited
Monsanto Canada Inc.
The Montreal Exchange
Montreal Trust
Moore Corporation Limited
Morgan Stanley Canada Inc.
Hugh C. Morris, Q.C.
Munich Reinsurance Company of Canada
The Mutual Life Assurance Company of
    Canada
National Trust
Nesbitt Burns
E.P. Neufeld
Newcourt Credit Group Inc.

Noma Industries Limited
Noranda Forest Inc.
Noranda Inc.
Northwood Pulp and Timber Limited
NOVA Corporation
Onex Corporation
Ontario Hydro
The Oshawa Group Limited
Katsuhiko Otaki
James S. Palmer
PanCanadian Petroleum Limited
Pembina Corporation
Petro-Canada
Philips, Hager & North Investment
    Management Ltd.
Pirie Foundation
Les Placements T.A.L. Ltée.
Placer Dome Inc.
Frank Potter
Patricia Pouliquen
Power Corporation of Canada
Pratt & Whitney Canada Inc.
Price Waterhouse
J. Robert S. Prichard
Procor Limited
ProGas Limited
QUNO Corporation
RBC Dominion Securities Inc.
Redpath Industries Limited
Henri Remmer
Retail Council of Canada
Richardson Greenshields
    of Canada Limited
R.T. Riley
Gordon Ritchie
Robin Hood Multifoods Inc.
Rogers Communications Inc.
J. Nicholas Ross, C.A.
Rothschild Canada Limited
Royal Bank of Canada
ROYCO Hotels & Resorts
SNC Lavalin Group Inc.
St. Lawrence Cement Inc.
Samuel, Son & Co., Limited
Sandwell Inc.
Sanpalo Investments Corporation
Guylaine Saucier

André Saumier
Sceptre Investment Counsel
Dick Schmeelk
The S. Schulich Foundation
ScotiaMcLeod Inc.
Shirley B. Seward
Sharwood and Company
Shell Canada Limited
Sidbec-Dosco (Ispat) Inc.
Sierra Systems Consultants Inc.
Adrienne Delong Snow
Southam Inc.
Spar Aerospace Limited
Speirs Consultants Inc.
Philip Spencer, Q.C.
The Standard Life Assurance Company
Stelco Inc.
Sun Life Assurance Company of Canada
Suncor Inc.
Swiss Re Life Canada
Brook Taylor
TELUS Corporation
Laurent Thibault
Thornmark Corporation
3M Canada Inc.

The Toronto Dominion Bank
The Toronto Stock Exchange
Torstar Corporation
Tory Tory DesLauriers & Binnington
TransAlta Utilities Corporation
TransCanada PipeLines Limited
Trimac Limited
Trizec Corporation Ltd.
Robert J. Turner
Unilever Canada Limited
United Grain Growers Limited
Urgel Bourgie Limitée
Vancouver Stock Exchange
VIA Rail Canada Inc.
Viridian Inc.
J.H. Warren
West Fraser Timber Co. Ltd.
Westcoast Energy Inc.
Weston Forest Corporation
Alfred G. Wirth
M.K. Wong & Associates Ltd.
Fred R. Wright
Xerox Canada Inc.
Paul H. Ziff

Honorary Members

G. Arnold Hart
David Kirk

Paul H. Leman
J. Ross Tolmie, Q.C.